NETSUKE

NETSUKE

The Japanese Art of Miniature Carving

Matthew Welch and Sharen Chappell

THE
MINNEAPOLIS
INSTITUTE
OF ARTS

This publication was produced in conjunction with the exhibition
"Netsuke: The Japanese Art of Miniature Carving."

The Minneapolis Institute of Arts, Minneapolis, Minnesota
April 4–July 5, 1998

The Herbert F. Johnson Museum of Art, Cornell University,
Ithaca, New York
August 21–October 24, 1999

Edited by Sandra L. Lipshultz

Photographed by Gary Mortensen and Robert Fogt

Designed by MartinRoss Design

Production coordinated by Donald Leurquin

2400 Third Avenue South
Minneapolis, Minnesota 55404

Printed in Belgium

Library of Congress Catalog Card Number 98-68586
ISBN 0-912964-66-9

FOREWORD

In 1975, a group of dedicated netsuke collectors established what eventually became known as the International Netsuke Society to exchange information about netsuke and its related art forms. To that end, the society hosts biennial conventions and publishes a quarterly journal. As membership has grown, chapters have also been organized in New York, Chicago, Cleveland, Washington, D.C., San Francisco, Los Angeles, London, and Tokyo.

Since the opening of Japan to the West in the mid-19th century, the netsuke market has been dominated by private collectors. In fact, some of the finest netsuke holdings in the world remain in private hands. In the spirit of sharing those remarkable treasures with a broader public, members of the society generously agreed to cosponsor the current exhibition by lending more than three hundred objects for display. As a result, many of the works featured in "Netsuke: The Japanese Art of Miniature Carving" are being shown and published for the very first time.

The exhibition and catalogue also represent a rare collaboration between a public museum and a private individual. Matthew Welch, curator of Japanese and Korean art at The Minneapolis Institute of Arts, and Sharen Chappell, an internationally known netsuke expert and former president of the society, combined their expertise to organize the exhibition on view and to write about the objects for the catalogue.

Moreover, the exhibition is remarkable for its great breadth. Works were selected for their quality and variety, thus providing a rich experience for both connoisseurs and initiates. An earnest attempt was also made to represent the entire history of netsuke production, from its beginnings in the 17th century with native carvers to its continuing vitality today with Japanese and Western artists alike. In the process, many compelling themes have emerged, including the Japanese reverence for the natural world, their abiding humor and wit, and an unflagging love of myths and legends. The catalogue also provides valuable insights into the historical and social context of netsuke making and details shifts in style and fashion that occurred over four centuries. As importantly, the final outcome not only tells the story of this spectacular art but provides something for everybody. It has been said that a good netsuke both amazes and amuses. This undertaking does just that by educating and entertaining the interested viewer.

Jay E. Hopkins, M.D.
President
International Netsuke Society

Acknowledgments

My deepest gratitude goes to the lenders to the exhibition. Not only did they loan their treasures for display but allowed them to be gone for an extended period. Many also generously contributed money to help print the catalogue. Donations to produce the book were also received from Mrs. Raymond Bushell, Denise Cohen, Michael and Lucy Foster, Jairus Hammond, Dr. and Mrs. James C. Hunt, Armin Müller and Lynn Richardson, Daniel and Fala Powers, Ted and Carolyn Schmidt, Michael Spindel, and Catherine S. Usibelli. As copublisher, Jeffery Moy of Paragon Publishing in Chicago deserves special recognition as well.

The realization of the exhibition and its accompanying catalogue has also depended on the dedication, talents, and generosity of many people. I would like to thank Sharen Chappell, former president of the International Netsuke Society, for her hard work and expertise. Without her participation, this project would not have reached fruition. I am deeply indebted to Dr. Jay Hopkins, the netsuke society's current president, for his unwavering enthusiasm and support, especially early on when funding for the catalogue seemed unobtainable. I also thank Marty Skoro and Ross Rezac of MartinRoss Design for their handsome layout of the book.

I would like to acknowledge several members of the Institute's staff as well. I am grateful to Sandra L. Lipshultz for her meticulous and sensitive editing; Gary Mortensen and Robert Fogt for their outstanding photography; Donald Leurquin for ably coordinating the catalogue production; Roxanne Ballard for elegantly designing the exhibition at the Minneapolis venue; and, as always, the museum's registrars and exhibition technicians for installing the show with painstaking care and efficiency.

Matthew Welch
Curator of Japanese and Korean Art
The Minneapolis Institute of Arts

Lenders to the Exhibition

Raymond and Virginia Atchley

Susan V. Atchley

Dr. and Mrs. Neil Barton

David and Margaret Burditt

Sharen T. Chappell

Neil and Sue Davey

Stephen Gardner

Dr. and Mrs. Robert Goodale

John and Donnie Hawley

Dr. and Mrs. Jay E. Hopkins

Kimberly Hopkins

Robert and Miriam Kinsey

Brooksie Koopman

Donald and Wanda Moyer

Mr. and Mrs. William S. Phillips

Akiko Sako

Norman L. Sandfield

June H. Schuerch

Mary A. Sherf

Richard R. Silverman

James J. Staggs

Dr. and Mrs. James Standefer

Masako Takayasu

Masanori Watanabe

Dr. and Mrs. Arthur J. Weiss

廣貞
金花堂

Before Western-style clothing became popular in the late 19th century, Japanese men wore kimonos with narrow cloth sashes that tied in the back. During the Edo, or Tokugawa, period (1600–1868), it became customary for them to carry a variety of personal belongings as well. Because kimonos had no pockets, such items as moneybags, tobacco pouches, lacquered cases for medicines or seals (inrō), and even small writing sets were suspended from braided silk cords. To prevent the cord from slipping—and causing the *sagemono*, or "hanging things," from falling to the ground—a toggle, or *netsuke*, was attached to the opposite end. This toggle rode on top of the sash, holding the *sagemono* in place.

Usually, artists made netsuke from wood or ivory, but they also sought out more exotic materials, like stag antler, boar tusk, horn, coral, and amber. A master carver could even transform fruit pits or walnuts into extraordinary objets d'art. At the height of netsuke production during the early 19th century, artists depicted hundreds of subjects, from the transcendent to the mundane. With great originality and technical skill, they carved legendary beasts and beings, Buddhist and Taoist deities, historical heroes, humble laborers, animals, birds, plants, fruit, and flowers. While some netsuke reflected the conservative tendencies of Japan's ruling elite, others depicted the earthy, sometimes lewd, tastes of a new class of wealthy commoners.

Because of their great variety and remarkable craftsmanship, netsuke quickly became popular with European and American collectors after Japan's 1868 "opening" to the West. Interest has remained strong throughout this century for Western and Japanese collectors alike, encouraging contemporary carvers to create designs that owe as much to tradition as to their own unique sensibilities.

During the Edo period, several distinct types of netsuke evolved and were often produced simultaneously. Regardless of type, however, artists were challenged to make designs that were both inventive and functional. To not be encumbrances, netsuke needed to be small and easy to wear. Even when netsuke shaped like standing figures became popular during the first half of the 18th century, sometimes reaching lengths of twelve centimeters, their profiles were always slender and never bulky. Regardless of the material used, the surface of a netsuke had to be smoothly polished so it could be easily pushed through the folds of the sash without snagging its fine fabric or the kimono. Holes (*himotoshi*) to accommodate the cord also had to be carefully placed so the netsuke's position on the sash would show it to good advantage and not be uncomfortable for the wearer. Poorly placed *himotoshi*, for

Opposite
Katsuma Gengobei in the play *Godairiki*
Color woodblock print
Mid-19th century
Signed: *Hironobu* (active 1851–70)

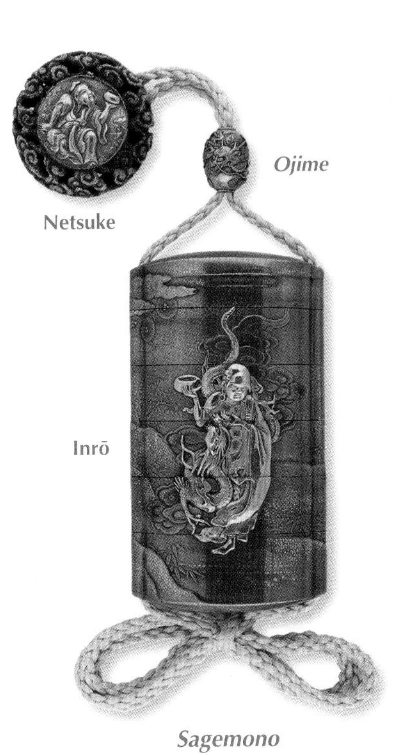

Inrō, netsuke, and *ojime* with Handaka theme
Inrō: wood, lacquer, and gold
Late 18th century
Signed: *Hasegawa Shigeyoshi* (Kajikawa school)
Netsuke disk: gold
Signed: *Masayoshi* (school unknown)
Netsuke bowl: stag antler
Late 19th century
Signed: *Tōkoku* (Tokyo school)
Ojime: gold
Late 19th century
Unsigned

example, might cause the netsuke to fall forward or tilt to one side. As importantly, netsuke needed to be durable. The material and design had to be structurally stable enough to be repeatedly worn and handled. Exploring the nuances of a netsuke's surface through blind touch, in fact, remains one of the great joys of this unique art form.

Manjū netsuke, so-called because they resemble soft, rounded confections made from glutinous rice, were one of the most popular and enduring forms. Usually fashioned from ivory, *manjū* netsuke can be solid or consist of two hollowed halves fitted together. Depending on the design, the cord could be fastened to the *manjū* netsuke in a variety of ways. Sometimes, it was tied to a small metal ring attached to the netsuke's back. With hollow *manjū*, the cord might pass through an eyelet hidden inside. Or, a plug with a hole drilled through its shank could be inserted into the *manjū*, allowing the cord to pass through the shank while emerging on the other side. The broad surface of the *manjū* netsuke's front provided artists with ample area for engraved designs or relief carving. During the mid-18th century, the artist Ryūsa expanded the repertoire by creating hollow *manjū* with elaborate carved openwork.

Because of their disk shape, *kagamibuta* netsuke resemble *manjū* netsuke, but actually consist of a low, circular bowl fitted with a lid (usually metal). The cord is tied to an eyelet on the underside of the lid. Artists frequently embellished *kagamibuta* lids with etched or repoussé designs. They often carved the surrounding bowl as well, establishing a dramatic "frame" for the central image.

Long, narrow netsuke are known as *sashi*, from the verb *sashi-komu*, meaning "to insert." Unlike conventional netsuke, *sashi* netsuke were tucked between the sash and the kimono and thus were more discreet accessories. Artists usually integrated the openings for the cord into the netsuke's design rather than drilling holes into these attenuated forms that might compromise their structural integrity. *Obi-hasami* are similar to *sashi* netsuke except they have hooked ends that cinch the sash and stay firmly in place.

The word *katabori* means "carved tusk or tooth." While suggesting the importance of ivory for traditional netsuke, the term came to designate representational netsuke carved fully in the round, regardless of material. Created as early as the mid-17th century, these miniature sculptures quickly became the most popular form of netsuke.

To keep the *katabori* netsuke functional, artists had to plan their compositions carefully. Certain details, like hands or horns, had to be worked so they would not break off or snag the fine material of the

Tobacco case, pipe holder, and pipe
Natural fungus, wood, metal, and lacquer
Late 19th century
Unsigned

kimono or the sash. If the cord could not pass through some natural opening, between an animal's leg, for instance, or through the crook of a person's arm, the artist had to drill holes in the piece that would not detract from its overall design.

With time, several distinct types of *katabori* netsuke developed. Some even had a secondary function in addition to their primary one as toggles. A hollowed portion in the design, for example, might serve as a small ashtray (cat. no. 76). Or, the base of the netsuke might be engraved with the owner's name or pseudonym and thus also be used as a seal. Some artists even outfitted their *katabori* netsuke with small movable parts for novel or "trick" effects. One finely crafted owl netsuke (cat. no. 232) has a tiny lever on its back that changes the bird's face from having wide "night eyes" to sleepy "day eyes."

Inrō, netsuke, and *ojime* with turtle theme
Wood
Early 19th century
Signed: *Hidari Issan*
(Iwashiro school)

Mask-shaped netsuke represent another important type of miniature carving. Japan's theatrical and dance traditions of Gigaku, Bugaku, Nō, and Kyōgen all involved masked performances. Some religious ceremonies, too, used masks to simulate the presence of divine beings. Before the Edo period, in fact, Buddhist statues and masks were the most significant forms of Japanese sculpture. Because of this, mask makers and Buddhist sculptors might have been among the earliest netsuke carvers.

During the Edo period, people from all classes of Japanese society enjoyed Nō and Kyōgen performances, not just the ruling elite as had previously. As a result, demand for mask-shaped netsuke grew. Usually, such netsuke faithfully reproduced well-known theatrical masks, but on a smaller scale (cat. no. 161). Theatergoers could purchase netsuke of their favorite characters, from auspicious spirits and tragic heroes to demons and divine animals. They could also choose a single netsuke carved with a jumble of many masks, a form that came into vogue during the 19th century (cat. no. 163).

The twelve animals of the Asian zodiac became a popular subject for 19th-century netsuke carvers as well. According to legend, the ancient Chinese emperor Huang Ti organized the lunar calendar into a sixty-year cycle made up of five, twelve-year units. A different animal governed each year in a twelve-year unit and gave people born in that year certain characteristics. Each day was also divided into twelve increments, with animals presiding over two-hour periods. Thus, the qualities of the animal associated with a person's time of birth intensified or lessened the traits related to the animal of one's year of birth.

Throughout Asia, people hired fortune-tellers and diviners to describe the particular personality resulting from the interaction of these two animals. They also sought help in determining the most compatible mates and the best times for weddings, funerals, and other major events. Netsuke customers tended to purchase the animal symbolizing their own birth year or the animal of the current year and often amassed a collection of netsuke representing all twelve animals.

"Found" objects also served as netsuke. In fact, the word *netsuke* means "attached root," suggesting the earliest netsuke might have actually been interesting pieces of tree or plant roots. Similarly, bits of coral, polished nuts, small gourds, empty turtle carapaces (cat. no. 186), and even the jawbones and fangs of wild animals (cat. no. 179) were used as netsuke and treasured by their owners for their exotic natural beauty.

Contemporary artists continue the grand traditions of netsuke carving established during the Edo period while bringing fresh ideas and unconventional techniques of their own to netsuke production. Since netsuke are now rarely worn, these artists have been freed from the limitations imposed by function. International restrictions on the use of ivory and other products from endangered species have been another catalyst for finding new and unusual materials. Along with the Japanese, carvers in the United States, Canada, Great Britain, and Australia have added unique subjects to the netsuke repertoire, including popular themes from their own countries. As a result, the practice of creating these exquisitely made miniatures, which began nearly four hundred years ago, continues to flourish today with remarkable vitality and imagination.

Inrō, netsuke, and *ojime* with dragon theme
Inrō: wood
Early 19th century
Signed: *Hidari Issan*
(Iwashiro school)
Netsuke: walnut
Late 19th century
Signed: *Kōzan*
(school unknown)
Ojime: fruit pit
Early 19th century
Signed: *Hidari Issan*
(Iwashiro school)

Notes to the Reader

In the text, Japanese pronunciations have been used for the names of Indian and Chinese religious figures. The original Sanskrit or Chinese pronunciation follows in parentheses.

The size of each netsuke is indicated by its greatest dimension only.

The majority of signatures listed represent art pseudonyms. When known, the artist's real name follows parenthetically in Japanese style, with the family name first and the given name second.

Broadly speaking, the catalogue has been arranged chronologically. Within each chapter, however, the objects have been presented thematically as follows: divine and supernatural figures, legendary heroes, humans, fantastic creatures, animals, nature studies, and inanimate objects.

When netsuke were first made is unknown. The practice of hanging objects from the belt, however, has a long history not limited to Japan. The Chinese, for example, attached pouches for flint and tinder, bags for perfume, and knives to their belts, as well as fabric or leather lappets decorated with sewn-on stone plaques and metal disks (Hutt, *Japanese Inrō*, pp. 14–15, and Arakawa, *Gō Collection*, pp. 187–88). From early times, Japanese warriors also tied the cinch cords of pouches to their sword hilts. Likewise, the custom of carrying inrō—small tiered cases for powdered medicine, family seals, and seal paste—probably began with Japan's military elite during the 16th century. These elegant, portable boxes often had lustrous lacquered surfaces and were derived from larger Chinese stacking cases.

Most likely, the earliest netsuke were "found" objects—an interesting section of root, a bit of coral, or a polished nut. But the first carved or turned netsuke were probably commissioned by Japan's warrior elite and made to accompany fine inrō. The development and proliferation of netsuke as a popular art form, however, is undoubtedly related to the rise of an affluent middle class.

During the early decades of the 17th century, the Tokugawa rulers enacted a series of political strategies that brought peace and prosperity to the country after nearly a hundred years of warfare. Japan's numerous feudal lords made their provincial castles administrative centers and required their samurai retainers to reside nearby. This, in turn, led to the migration of merchants, artists, and laborers to these castle towns, all hoping to earn a living catering to the needs of warriors and government officials. In fact, the phenomenal growth of these urban centers during the 1600s was unprecedented in Japanese history. By 1700, Osaka had nearly 300,000 residents, while Edo, the seat of shogunal authority, had more than one million, making it one of the world's largest cities.

With these burgeoning metropolises came the rise of a class of urban commoners, known as *chōnin*. *Chōnin* merchants grew rich providing goods and services to the inhabitants of these bustling cities. As the country gradually shifted from an agrarian barter system to a currency-based economy, *chōnin* rice brokers greatly profited by converting government rice stipends into cash. And when government subsidies became outpaced by inflation, a situation that began during the second half of the 17th century and plagued the remainder of the Tokugawa period, members of the privileged class borrowed from *chōnin* moneylenders at staggering interest rates.

However, the strict stratification of Japanese society prevented prosperous townsmen from advancing socially despite their enormous wealth. As a result, many pursued hedonistic pleasures and indulged in extravagant pastimes. By the middle of the 17th century, *chōnin*, as a dynamic cultural force in their own right, engendered art forms suited to their own particular needs and tastes.

Kabuki theater and puppet performances, for example, both developed as amusements for *chōnin* audiences. And the licensed pleasure quarters, walled enclaves of brothels and teahouses, allowed *chōnin* men to keep company with the most acclaimed women of the day and in so doing take pride in bettering their samurai superiors. Popular literature, too, glorified the lavish habits of wealthy commoners, who achieved stylish lifestyles notably at odds with their position in society. As early as the Kambun era (1661–73), this trend became pervasive, reaching its high point during the Genroku era (1688–1704).

With society becoming increasingly consumer-oriented, *chōnin* men found it convenient and necessary to have a number of items with them at all times. As coinage became standardized and money minted, a national currency was in place by 1636. In cities, business transactions were handled in cash, rather than in bartered goods. *Chōnin* merchants carried their money in small leather or fabric purses (*kinchaku*) and an increasing number of keys—to shops, warehouses, and money boxes. The popularity of tobacco, too, which had been introduced to Japan by Spanish and Portuguese traders during the late 17th century, required an easy means of carrying a pipe and a supply of loose tobacco. In addition, a variety of other consumer goods expressly designed to be easily portable were made, including *yatate* (miniature writing sets), abacuses, and ash receptacles for smoking.

An unusual netsuke was just one of many details that would have allowed a fashion-conscious man-about-town to impress his friends and acquaintances with his taste and wealth.

Literary and pictorial sources make clear that such early *sagemono*, like *kinchaku*, inrō, and tobacco pouches, were fastened to silk cords that were tied to metal or ivory rings, known as *obikuruma*, through which the sash passed as well (Arakawa, *Gō Collection*, pp. 193–99). These *sagemono* cords could also be attached to smaller, thicker rings that hung over the sash and functioned as counter weights (Arakawa, *Gō Collection*, pp. 200–201). *Manjū* netsuke, with their discreetly hidden eyelets for the cord, probably developed from these early rings and became prevalent during the second quarter of the 17th century.

Katabori netsuke, carved fully in the round, must have followed soon thereafter. Two references from fictional literature suggest as much. Ihara Saikaku's *Kōshoku ichidai onna* (Life of an Amorous Woman) from 1686 mentions an antique shop with a variety of goods displayed in the window, including a netsuke with a Chinese-lion design (Arakawa, *Gō Collection*, p. 196). The next year, Saikaku published *Nanshoku ōkagami* (Great Mirror of Love between Men), in which he depicted an aging homosexual as pathetic because of his hopelessly antiquated dress:

> The man, without one black hair on his head, wore a striped Takijima kimono and plum-colored *haori* jacket fastened high on his chest with a cord. He carried a short sword decorated with walnut half-shells. From his sash hung an old-fashioned inrō and a tanned leather *kinchaku* held in place by a netsuke of a figure pulling a horse. It is unthinkable that anyone with such an unrefined appearance would offer his heart to a male prostitute.

Since Saikaku presented both of the netsuke in these accounts as being outmoded, it can be inferred that *katabori* netsuke were being carved at least as early as the mid-1660s or 1670s.

While the desire to carry a variety of personal effects precipitated the functional genesis of *sagemono,* mere convenience alone does not explain the growth of netsuke production. It seems more likely that netsuke—and *sagemono* ensembles in general—provided men with a novel way to accessorize their kimonos.

In this regard, an unusual netsuke was just one of many details that would have allowed a fashion-conscious man-about-town to impress his friends and acquaintances with his taste and wealth. In Ihara Saikaku's 1682 *Kōshoku ichidai otoku* (Life of an Amorous Man), for instance, the dissolute hero, Yonosuke, dresses fancily to visit the famous Kyoto courtesan Kaoru:

> His undergarment was scarlet, and his robe, tied with a sash of light gray faux brocade, was yellow crepe de chine decorated with the scattered crests of his favorite courtesans. His *haori* jacket was black camlet with a striped velvet lining. He wore a long sword of the type seen in popular places on pretentious men-about-town, with an indigo sharkskin scabbard and a small antique iron sword guard and on a long hilt, four gold ornaments. Suspended by an interwoven braid of lavender and gray was a flat inrō and a colored leather coin purse, each with an agate *ojime,* held in place by a fine carved netsuke of rare imported wood.

Unfortunately, the lack of securely datable early netsuke makes it difficult to fully understand the nature of netsuke production during the 17th century (Kurstin, "Seventeenth-Century Netsuke," pp. 44–57). Literary descriptions of netsuke also tend to be brief and lacking in potentially helpful details. Genre paintings of the period make it evident that *manjū* netsuke were commonplace, but the degree to which they had surface carving is hard to surmise. Since netsuke artists did not begin to sign their works until the mid-18th century, little about the craftsmen before that time is known.

Nevertheless, a group of netsuke has been identified that predates the powerfully carved figures from the early 18th century. Despite the flourishing of Japan's plebeian class and the emergence of an indigenous popular culture, these early netsuke often reflect time-honored subjects derived from China. Shōki, the demon queller (cat. no. 1), for example, is a legendary Chinese folk hero, and the eccentric Hotei (cat. no. 3), a Chinese Buddhist monk. Early animal netsuke also frequently depict nonnative species (cat. no. 7) or mythical beasts of Chinese origin (cat. no. 6). Stylistically, these early netsuke usually have bold overall designs with minimal surface details and embellishments. They also tend to be somewhat bulky in scale. Nonetheless, they are always refreshing in their forthright presentation of subject and form.

1

Shōki, 17th century
Ivory; 13.2 cm
Unsigned

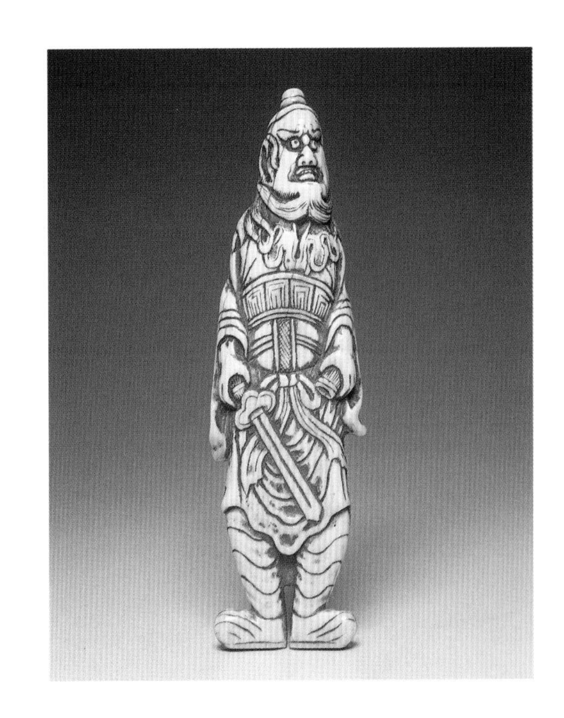

According to Chinese legend, Shōki (Chung K'uei) was a T'ang dynasty scholar who, though he passed the imperial examinations, was denied a government position because of his ungainly appearance. In despair, he dashed his head against the palace steps. When the emperor Ming-huang learned of the tragic incident, he ordered an official burial for the scholar. Later, Shōki's appreciative spirit appeared before the emperor and vowed to rid the land of evil demons for all eternity. This netsuke portrays the ever vigilant Shōki with his large, watchful eyes and unsheathed sword. The figure's thin, curved proportions suggest it was carved from a piece of ivory taken from the base of a tusk. During the 17th century, ivory was extremely rare, and artists creatively used every available part of the precious commodity.

2

Demon on a rock, 17th century
Ivory; 5 cm
Unsigned

In traditional Chinese and Japanese mythology, *oni*, demons with claws for fingers and toes, carry out the harsh punishments decreed by the King of Hell. Since the 14th century, Japanese artists have delighted in portraying the fiendish monsters going gleefully about their grisly work. In this netsuke, a well-muscled *oni* looks down from his perch on a rock and smiles malevolently. Typical of some old ivory, the piece has a deep orange patina that adds to the *oni*'s association with the fiery depths of hell.

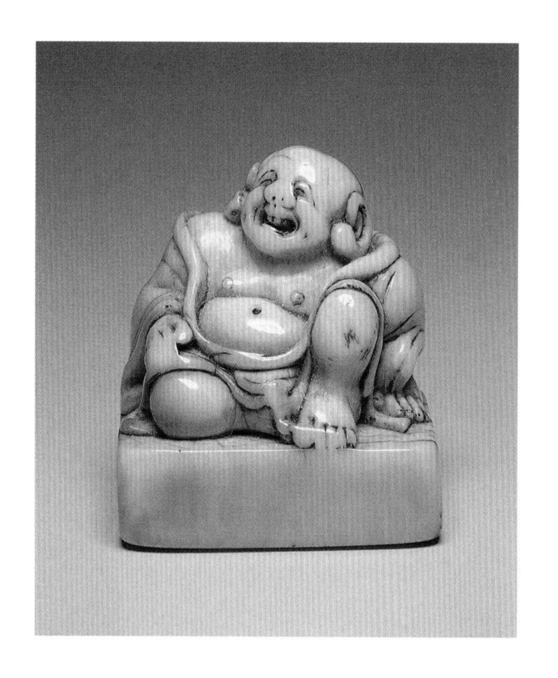

3

Hotei, 17th century

Ivory; 4 cm

Unsigned

An eccentric Buddhist priest who lived in China during the 9th century, Hotei (Pu-tai) was usually portrayed as a happy wanderer unconcerned with social conventions or material wealth. As such, he became a favorite subject for Zen ink painters, who saw him as the personification of nonattachment. Later, however, Hotei became popularized as one of the Seven Gods of Good Fortune, and his large stomach and traveler's sack came to symbolize material abundance. This netsuke of him has a square base, which was meant to be carved with the owner's name and used as a seal.

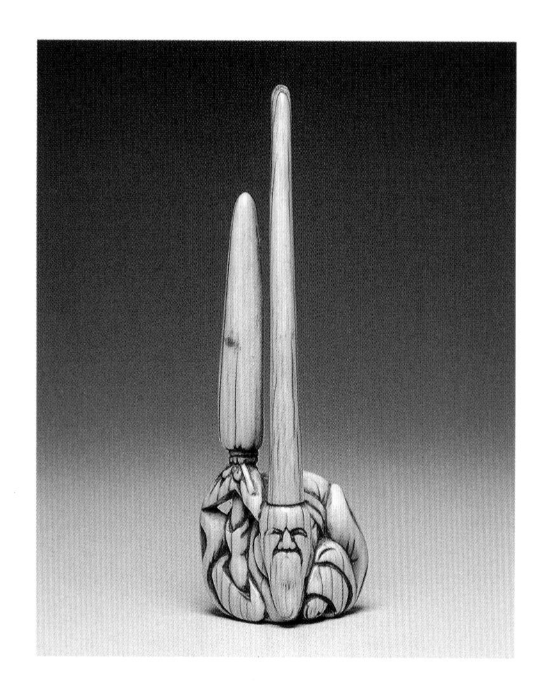

4

Umbrella bearer, 17th century

Stag antler; 10 cm

Unsigned

When feudal lords and high-ranking aristocrats traveled, they were accompanied by many attendants. This netsuke portrays a kneeling umbrella bearer, waiting until his services are needed. The artist humorously elongated his lacquered hat to reflect the proportions of the umbrella.

5

Winged dragon, 17th century
Marine ivory; 4 cm
Unsigned, possibly Chinese

The Chinese also used small toggles to secure personal objects to their belts. In both subject matter and style, this winged dragon resembles such Chinese toggles and might have been made on the mainland.

6

Shishi, 17th century
Wood; 7 cm
Unsigned

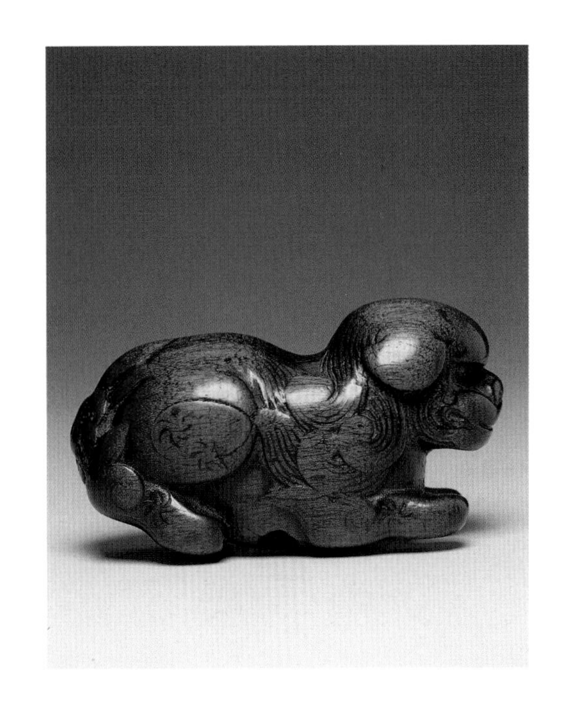

Although lions were not native to China, their pelts were probably first brought there by Indian and Middle Eastern traders. Early on, Chinese artists made lions into magical beasts with luxurious, curling manes and tails. In both China and Japan, large-scale stone sculptures of lions (as emblems of strength) often flanked the entrances to temples. This early netsuke resembles such a lion with its massive form and bold, stylized mane. Made from wood, it is a rare example from an era when carvers preferred working in ivory.

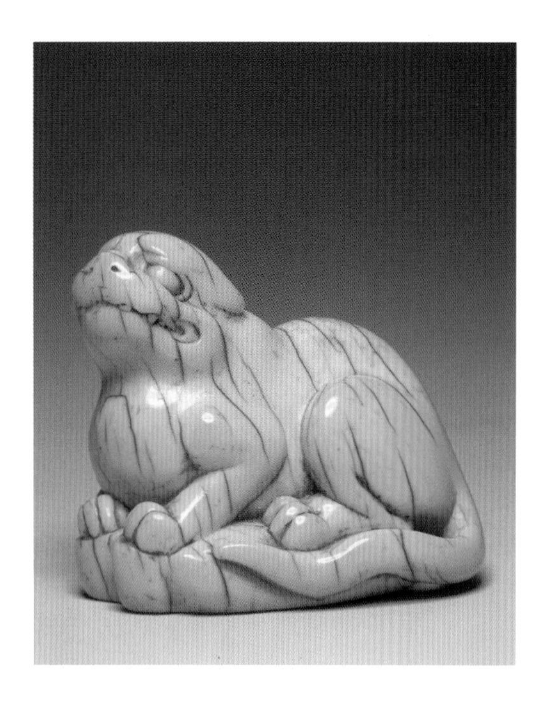

7

Tiger, 17th century
Ivory; 5.2 cm
Unsigned

As in the West, tigers symbolize power and strength in Asia. The posture of this beast, crouching on a plinth, resembles the enormous stone tigers used as guardians at palaces and temples. The work's simple design, spare details, and smooth surface characterize very early netsuke. The custom of inlaying eyes with dark pieces of horn or coral did not begin until the middle of the 18th century, thus accounting for this tiger's "blank" gaze.

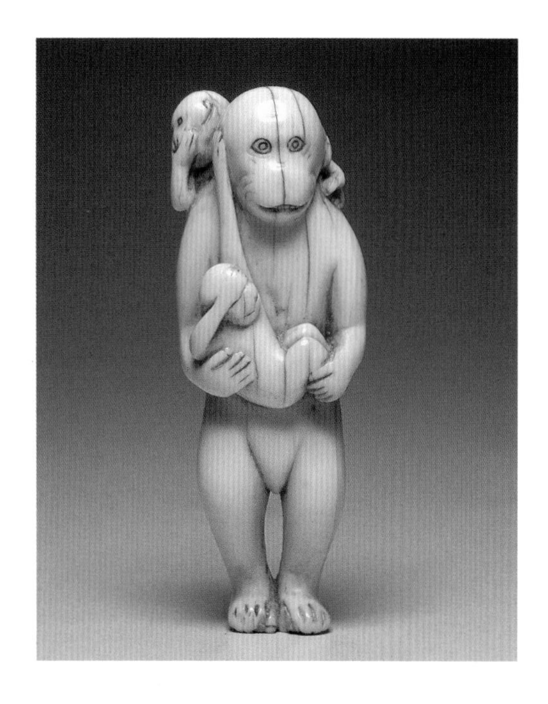

8

Monkey and young, 17th century
Ivory; 7 cm
Unsigned

This netsuke illustrates the three virtuous monkeys who "hear no evil, see no evil, speak no evil." One young monkey covers its eyes; the other, its mouth, and together they cover their mother's ears. Like other early netsuke, this work has been boldly designed and executed. Rather than realistically depicting the monkeys' fur, as would become popular in the 18th century, the artist rendered the animals as a composite of smoothly geometric forms. This approach, together with the cool creaminess of the ivory, makes for an object of great tactile appeal.

Despite the flourishing of *chōnin* culture, netsuke made during the early to mid-18th century reflected a continuing preference for "things Chinese," especially for portrayals of Buddhist deities, Taoist immortals, and mythical beasts. Other art forms, like popular literature, Kabuki theater, and ukiyo-e prints and paintings, all celebrated the newly emerging middle class by depicting their reigning beauties, spendthrift dandies, and cunning shopkeepers. In this light, netsuke production during the early to mid-18th century seems oddly anachronistic in terms of subject matter. A number of reasons, however, account for the tenacious popularity of Chinese-inspired themes.

During the early 17th century, the Tokugawa government adopted Neo-Confucianism as its ruling ideology, helping to ensure that Japanese scholars continued to look to China for philosophical leadership. This brand of Confucianism, first promulgated by the 12th-century Chinese sage Chu Hsi, attached metaphysical significance to "right" conduct within relationships, especially between rulers and subjects, husbands and wives, and parents and children. Thus, a breach in proper conduct was tantamount to disrupting the cosmic order. As a result, the creed helped legitimize and preserve Tokugawa rule through an unquestioning loyalty and deference to its authority.

Seventeenth-century Japanese scholars of Neo-Confucianism tended to come from the samurai class, eventually abandoning their swords for bureaucratic positions in the government or to set up their own schools. By the early 18th century, however, commoners were studying Confucian classics and Chinese poetry at private academies and local temple schools, which were often staffed by samurai-scholars. Through his Kyōhō Reforms, the eighth Tokugawa shogun, Yoshimune (1684–1751), attempted to rectify the country's financial and agrarian problems by urging all levels of society to live a model Confucian lifestyle of frugality and restraint. To this end, commoners were allowed to attend lectures at the Seidō, the shogunal academy in Yushima, for the first time in 1717 (Hall, *Early Modern Japan*, p. 455). Soon thereafter, the government published Confucian textbooks expressly for commoners. Even in Osaka, a bastion of intense mercantile activity, a commoners' school of Chinese studies opened in 1724 (Hall, *Early Modern Japan*, p. 725). These events all helped foster a broad-based interest in Chinese culture that flourished during the 18th century.

At the same time, the Kano school, which specialized in Chinese-style landscapes, bird-and-flower compositions, and figural themes, remained unrivaled in Japan for its widespread influence. Starting in the 15th century, artists of this school enjoyed hereditary status as official artists of the shogunate. During the 17th century, Kano masters established ateliers in Edo to cater to the central authority, while branch schools in the provinces drew support from feudal lords.

In addition, *machi-eshi*, town painters trained in the Kano manner but not considered official members of the school, also practiced throughout Japan. Many artists from other schools and disciplines began their studies in Kano studios as well. This tradition undoubtedly influenced early 18th-century netsuke carvers, who favored Chinese themes and probably used Kano painting manuals as their models.

Netsuke from the first half of the 18th century often possess great elegance and grandeur. Artists achieved these qualities by elongating the netsuke's proportions and carving the material to a fairly narrow cross-section. This can be seen especially in the tall, standing figures, which often taper down to fairly small feet. While the upright nature of bipedal subjects naturally lent themselves to this treatment, quadrupeds and mythical beasts must have presented carvers with far greater compositional challenges. But by bunching the hooves together, as if the animal were balancing on a ball (cat. nos. 20 and 32), artists created a similar tapered gracefulness. The attenuated proportions of these pieces gave them a higher point of gravity, often with the bulk of the work in the upper half. Usually, the *himotoshi* were drilled into this upper portion, allowing the netsuke to extend over the sash, and were uneven in size, with one opening much larger to discreetly accommodate the knot.

Many ivory netsuke produced during the first half of the 18th century also have an overall triangular shape (cat. nos. 23, 31, and 39). This distinctive profile probably resulted from the prevalent method of sectioning tusks (Hopkins, "Early Elephant Ivory Netsuke," pp. 7–18). Thus, the netsuke carvers' desire to leave as much of the precious material intact caused them to creatively adapt their designs to the general shape of rough-cut ivory.

Despite their graceful forms, early to mid-18th century netsuke are often powerfully expressive as well. The smooth planes and tentatively incised surfaces of earlier netsuke gave way in these examples to deep undercutting and superbly rendered details. These techniques, however, were not necessarily used for a heightened realism, but rather to contribute to the otherworldly grandeur and often bizarre nature of their subjects. The agitated and undulating robes of Taoist immortals, for instance, suggest their superhuman energy, whereas their heavy brows and bulging eyes convey the intensity of their mental acuity (cat. nos. 9, 10, 13, and 16). Similarly, other details, like the tight curls of a *baku*'s mane, accentuate the fanciful appearance of the creature while also evoking its imaginary nature (cat. nos. 40, 74, and 75).

The smooth planes and tentatively incised surfaces of earlier netsuke gave way to deep undercutting and superbly rendered details.

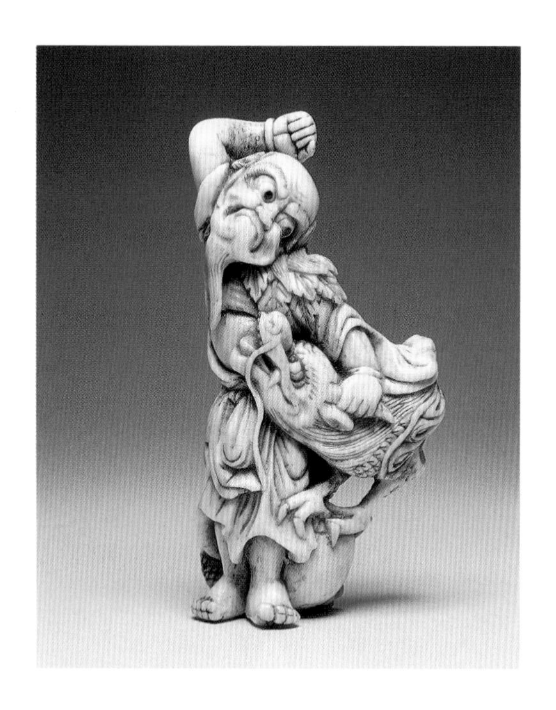

9

Chinnan, early 18th century

Stag antler with horn inlay; 9.5 cm

Signed: *Mototada* (school unknown)

Asian artists usually represented the Chinese Taoist immortals as ascetic mountain men with wild features, unkempt hair and clothing, and accompanied by extraordinary animals. The Taoist immortal Chinnan (Ch'en-nan) had the power to call forth a rain dragon from his begging bowl. The artist Mototada skillfully used a piece of branched antler for this netsuke of the sage. He carved Chinnan's head and upraised arm from one branch and formed the dragon's taut body from the smaller branch. Chinnan subdues the powerful beast by grasping its horn with one hand and preparing to strike its snout with the other. Mototada's masterful rendering of the immortal's leaf cape, fluttering robes, and expressively bulging eyes makes the composition even more dynamic.

10

Chinnan, early 18th century

Ivory; 13.5 cm

Unsigned

Like catalogue number 9, this netsuke represents the Taoist immortal Chinnan (Ch'en-nan) with his rain dragon. The unknown maker here created a marvelous interplay between the tense, motionless sage and the writhing animal, whose mischievous face glowers as its tail whips up behind its master. For its early date, the composition is quite daring, with Chinnan's beard and the dragon's tail carved free from the main piece of ivory. The gap between the sage's sleeve and his body forms a natural *himotoshi*.

11
Ikkaku, early 18th century
Wood; 13.3 cm
Unsigned

A Taoist immortal and a wizard of great power, Ikkaku can be identified by the horn that grows from his forehead. According to legend, he lived deep in the mountains of India. One rainy day, he slipped and fell while walking along a steep path. Angered, he imprisoned the rain dragons in a large jar, which led to a widespread drought. The rain dragons were freed, however, when Ikkaku lost his magical powers by succumbing to a beautiful woman. Here, he carries the temptress on his back, while tenderly reaching to caress her hand. His apron of leaves, emaciated chest, and haggard features suggest the hardships of his ascetic existence.

12
Tekkai, early 18th century
Wood; 10.5 cm
Unsigned

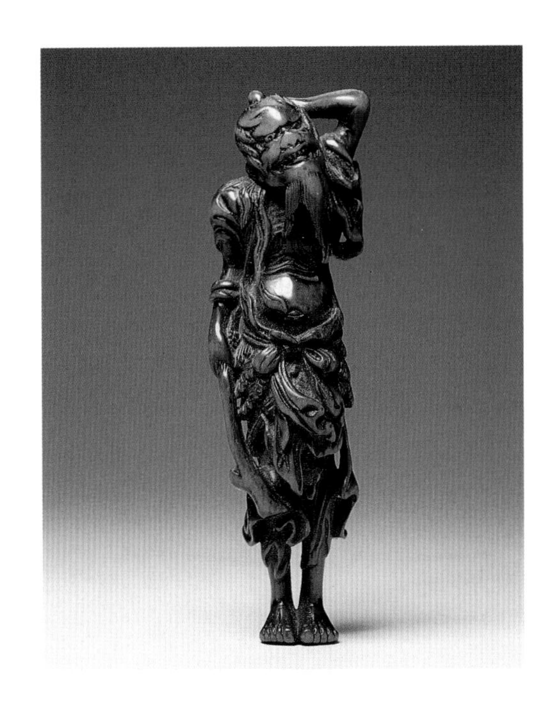

The Chinese Taoist immortal Tekkai (T'ieh-kuai) had the unusual ability to exhale his soul from his body, thus allowing it to freely travel great distances. Once when Tekkai's soul had been gone for several days, his young disciple assumed that the immortal had abandoned his mortal body, so he cremated it. When Tekkai's soul finally returned, it had no place to reside and had to settle for the dead body of a lame beggar. Hence, as can be seen in this netsuke, Tekkai (literally "iron crutch") wears the beggar's tattered clothes and uses his crutch. He holds his hand to his head, conveying his bewilderment at having lost his rightful body. Masterfully carved, the high relief of the fluttering drapery serves to enliven the miniature's overall composition.

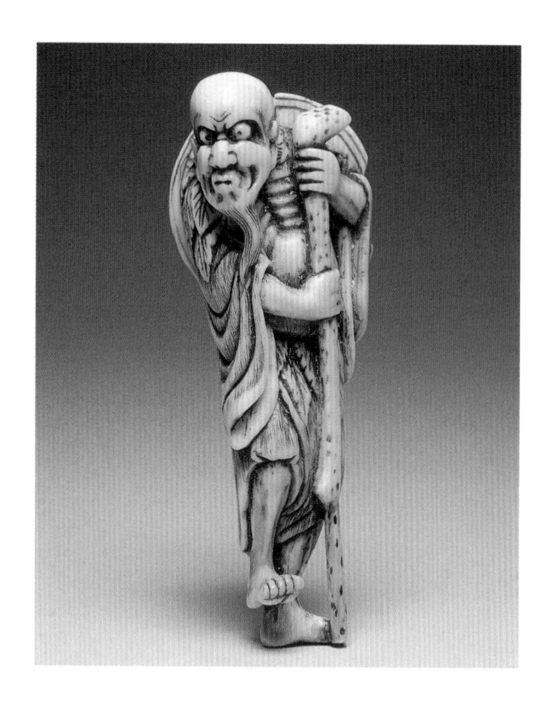

13

Tekkai, early 18th century
Ivory; 8 cm
Unsigned

Like catalogue number 12, this powerful figure represents Tekkai (T'ieh-kuai), a Taoist immortal forced to occupy the body of a dead lame beggar. Typical of early netsuke representing ascetics, relatively large orbs of ivory were left for the eyes, while the surrounding area was carved away to suggest deep sockets. This technique gave these bizarre sages appropriately fierce expressions that accorded well with their tortured bodies and tattered clothing. The unknown artist here animated the design further by having the figure twist in space and lift his leg, as if to take a step. To not interrupt the composition, the maker also cleverly integrated the *himotoshi*, placing one opening beneath Tekkai's sedge hat and the other in the loose folds of his left sleeve.

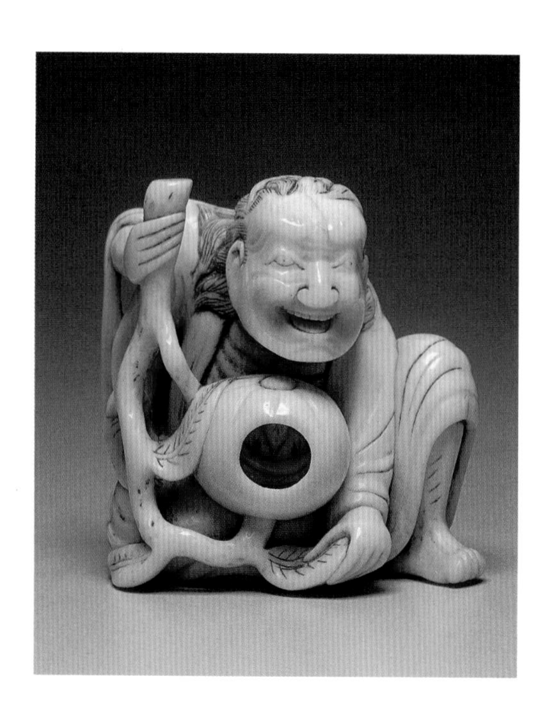

14

Tōbōsaku, early 18th century
Ivory; 5 cm
Unsigned

The Taoist immortal Tōbōsaku (Tung Fang Shu) was a court advisor to the Han dynasty emperor Wu Ti. According to legend, Tōbōsaku so wanted his contented life to continue that he stole magical peaches that gave the eater immortality. In this netsuke, he smiles broadly while holding a peach branch from the heavenly garden of goddess Seiōbo (Hsi Wang Mu). Depictions of this legend usually include a small figure inside the peach reading a handscroll to represent Tōbōsaku's previous life as a scholar. The artist skillfully disguised the triangular shape of the original rough-cut ivory by carving Tōbōsaku's raised arm and the peach branch in high relief with openwork. The figure's unusual, Medusalike hair accentuates his grotesquely grinning face.

15
Tōbōsaku, early 18th century
Ivory; 9.8 cm
Unsigned

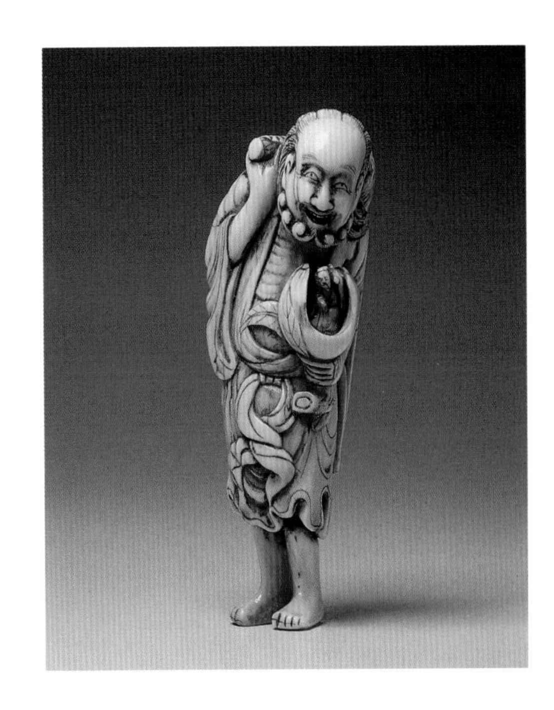

This Tōbōsaku (Tung Fang Shu) smiles broadly at having successfully stolen a peach of immortality (see cat. no. 14). Like other depictions of immortals, elements of the figure have been oddly stylized to suggest his otherworldly nature, including the symmetrical curls of his beard, the fanciful crisscross of his sash, and the undulating hem of his robe. The old scholar's newly found divinity has also been indicated by the *hossu,* the implement he holds in his right hand to gently brush away insects, thus demonstrating his respect for all forms of life. Despite these details, however, the artist imbued this Tōbōsaku with a beguiling humanity by rendering his face without the bulging eyes and exaggerated features typically given to such figures.

16
Taoist immortal and *minogame*, early 18th century
Stag antler with horn inlay; 10 cm
Attributed to Tomohisa (school unknown)

Taoist immortals (*sennin*) have supernatural powers and extraordinary animals as companions. Asians believe that tortoises live for a thousand years. Aquatic vegetation clings to the carapaces of the oldest, giving them sweeping trains. Because these trains resemble the straw raincoats (*mino*) worn by Japanese peasants, tortoises (*kame* or *game*) with this attribute came to be called *minogame,* or raincoat tortoises. As creatures of great age, *minogame* were apt companions for Taoist immortals. This netsuke shows a *minogame* playfully crawling over the shoulder of a *sennin,* who seems to grimace from the scratchy touch of the animal's claws. The artist cleverly used a piece of branched stag antler for his composition: he carved the tortoise and the figure's legs, torso, and head from the trunk of the antler and the immortal's sedge hat from a subsidiary branch.

17
Kanzan and Jittoku, early 18th century
Wood; 8 cm
Unsigned

The Chinese poet Kanzan (Han-shan) lived during the 7th century, and his verse is still admired today. Kanzan befriended the orphan Jittoku (Shih-te), who was raised in the Buddhist monastery of Kuo-ch'ing-ssu on Mount T'ien-t'ai. To earn his keep, Jittoku worked in the temple kitchen and saved scraps of food for Kanzan. Their lack of concern for material wealth and social conventions made them popular subjects for early Zen ink painters, who usually pictured them with unkempt hair and ragged clothing. In this unusual portrayal, one figure suggests the pair by holding two objects: a scroll, which alludes to Kanzan's poetry, and a broom, which Jittoku used to sweep the kitchen floor.

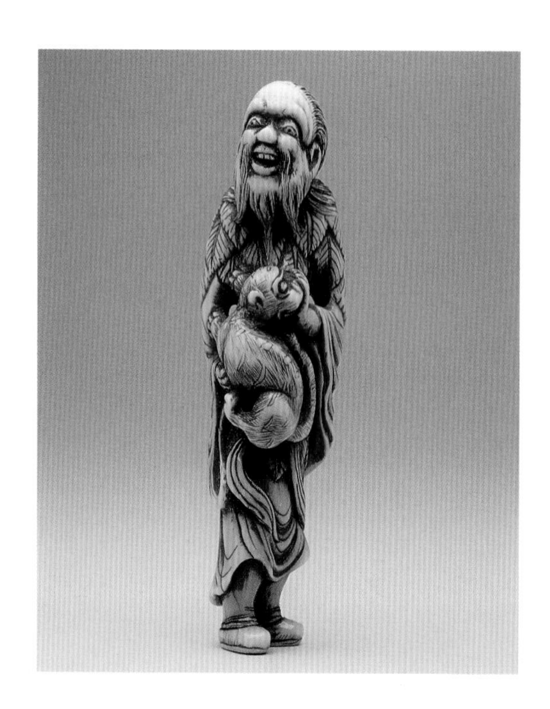

18
Bukan and tiger, mid-18th century
Ivory; 10.5 cm
Unsigned

According to tradition, the 7th-century Buddhist priest Bukan (Feng-kan) of Kuo-ch'ing-ssu temple on Mount T'ien-t'ai befriended the poet Kanzan (Han-shan) and the orphan Jittoku (Shih-te). Because of their lack of concern for material possessions and social standing, the three came to symbolize the Zen ideal of nonattachment. This netsuke shows Bukan reaching down to stroke the face of his unusual companion, a tiger, who has been whimsically represented as a house cat. For this composition, the artist used a triangular section of raw ivory, sculpting Bukan's back out of one flat side.

19

Bukan and tiger, early 18th century
Ivory; 8 cm
Unsigned

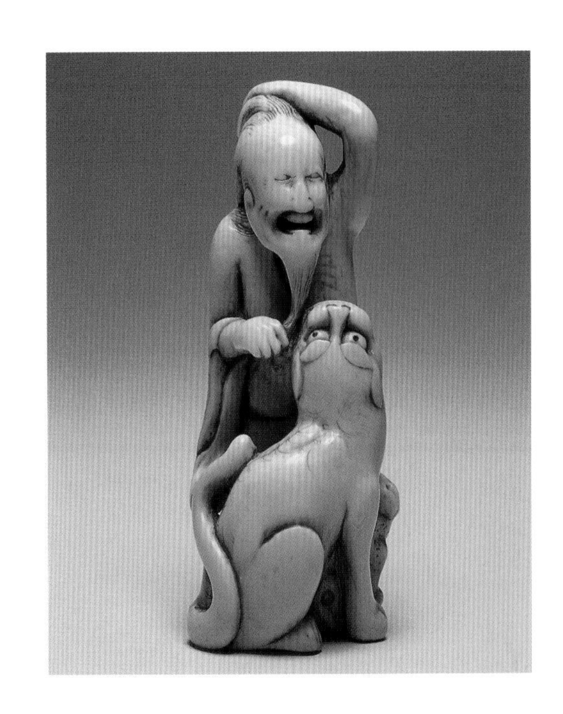

This smoothly carved Bukan and tiger dramatically contrasts with the previous example (cat. no. 18), which has crisply cut details. Although some of this effect may have resulted from wear, it also reflects the artist's desire to accentuate the quality of the ivory by creating a piece as compelling tactilely as it is visually. While the tiger here is proportionate in scale to the priest, it nevertheless behaves as playfully as a kitten, staring adoringly upward as Bukan holds his head and laughs.

20

Roshi riding an ox, early 18th century
Wood; 11.5 cm
Unsigned

According to tradition, the Chinese sage Roshi (Lao-tzu) wrote the *Tao Te Ching,* the philosophical basis for Taoism, which asserted that people should strive to live in harmony with the *tao,* the eternal and pervasive rhythm of nature. After completing his text, Roshi supposedly mounted an ox and left China for the West. This netsuke portrays the great man holding a scroll and cradling his head, as if deep in thought. Instead of portraying the ox with anatomical accuracy, the artist, like other early netsuke carvers, showed much more interest in creating a bold and elegant shape for his miniature.

21

***Kagamibuta* netsuke with Daruma**, early 18th century
Pottery and ironwood; 4 cm diam.
Signed: *Kan* (Ritsuo)

In the early 6th century, the Indian prince Daruma (Bodhidharma) traveled from India to China to spread the word of the Buddha. By emphasizing seated meditation, Daruma established the Zen (Ch'an) sect in Asia. Artists usually portray him wearing the red robes of an Indian holy man. In this netsuke, he also holds a fly whisk to gently brush away annoying insects, thus abiding by the Buddhist laws against taking life. A versatile artist, Ritsuo had equal facility in several media, including wood, clay, ivory, and lacquer. He excelled at manipulating lacquer to imitate the texture and quality of other materials, like ceramic tiles and ink sticks. In this netsuke, he fashioned the disk from ceramic, which he pigmented with lacquer. To provide a contrasting texture, the surrounding bowl has been carved from ironwood.

22

Shōki and demon, early 18th century
Ivory; 5.3 cm
Unsigned

In addition to emphasizing the fierce determination and power of the demon queller Shōki (Chung K'uei; see cat. no. 1), artists also delighted in showing imps getting the better of him. Here, Shōki has been humbled by a brutish demon, who has pulled off his loin cloth and left him naked and begging for mercy. The representation becomes humorous from the reversal of roles.

23

Shōki and demon, early 18th century
Ivory; 7 cm
Unsigned

In the 17th and 18th centuries, merchants cut their ivory into triangular cross sections before selling it. Netsuke artists, attempting to use as much of the precious material as possible, skillfully adapted their designs to this triangular shape. Here, the demon queller Shōki (Chung K'uei) tries to trap an imp beneath a sedge hat. During the struggle, the demon's head breaks the hat.

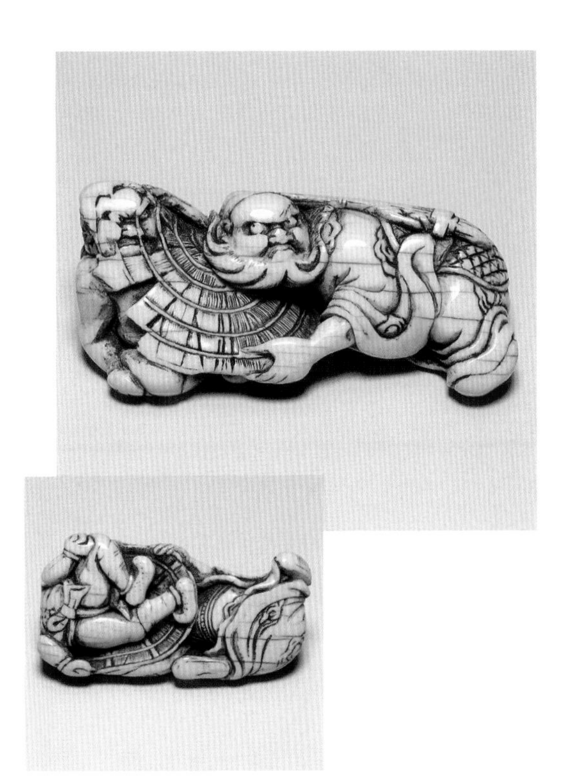

24

God of wind, early 18th century
Ivory; 4.3 cm
Unsigned

Asian artists have long personified such natural phenomena as wind and thunder. The gods of wind (*Fūjin*) and thunder (*Raijin*), which derived from Indian mythology, were subsumed into the Buddhist pantheon and pictured in Japanese sutras and wall paintings from an early date. They are usually shown as seminaked, heavily muscled demons with bulging eyes and flamelike hair. Like generic demons (*oni*), they also can have horns and claws. In this netsuke, *Fūjin* stands on a swirling cloud with his bag of winds, which he can release at whim.

25

Hotei with puppet, early 18th century
Wood; 8.5 cm
Unsigned

An eccentric Buddhist monk who lived during the 9th century, Ch'i-tz'u earned the nickname "pu-tai" (big bag or big belly) because of his large stomach and the cloth bag he carried. Zen painters were fond of picturing Pu-tai (Hotei in Japanese) as a wandering priest unconcerned with social conventions or material wealth. Because of his happy nature, he was also associated with children and often pictured as an oversized playmate. This netsuke cleverly varies that theme, showing Hotei playing with a puppet of a Chinese child.

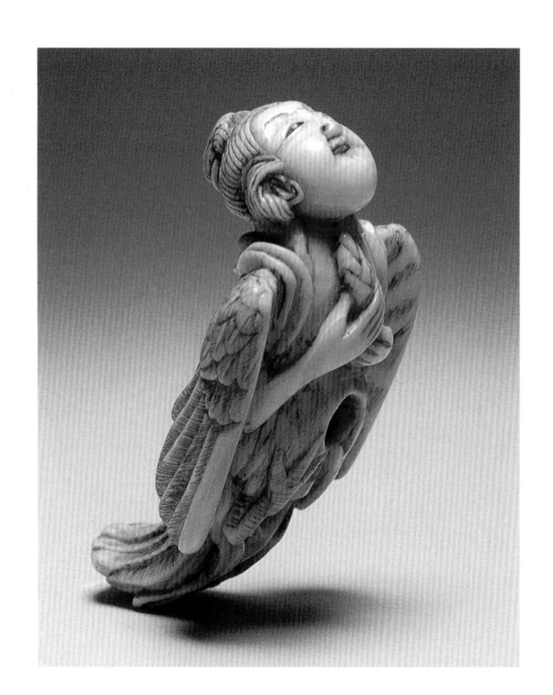

26

Karyōbinga, early 18th century
Ivory; 6.5 cm
Unsigned

The mythical *karyōbinga* has the head and torso of a human and the body of a bird. In Japan, it is associated with Buddhism and regarded as a celestial creature whose melodious voice is heard in Amida Buddha's Pure Land. Neither male nor female, it is usually shown with the elaborate coiffeur and sweet round face of a T'ang dynasty (618–906) aristocrat. It sometimes holds a panpipe or, as here, a lotus bud, symbolic of the purity of Buddhist teachings.

27

Dragon King's attendant with octopus, early 18th century
Boxwood; 11.4 cm
Unsigned

The Chinese believe that the Dragon King rules the seas from a magnificent palace deep beneath the waves. Part of his immense power, including his ability to control the tides, comes from a magic jewel he possesses. According to legend, the Dragon King gave his magical orb to Takeuchi-no-Sukune, prime minister of the late 4th-century empress Jingō. This netsuke portrays the Dragon King's attendant, tensely posed and holding the jewel. An octopus rides on his head, its tentacles draping down his back.

28

Dragon King's attendant, mid-18th century
Wood; 12 cm
Unsigned

Similar in conception and expression to catalogue number 27, this attendant also holds the Dragon King's jewel. While the top of his head is bald, the figure has long, tentaclelike locks of hair cascading down his back, a clever allusion to his usual companion—an octopus.

29

Kiyohime, early 18th century
Ivory with inlay; 8.2 cm
Unsigned

In the popular Nō play *Dojoji*, a young woman named Kiyohime becomes infatuated with Anchin, a handsome monk whose repeated refusals only enflame her passions. Eventually, Kiyohime chases Anchin to Dojoji temple, where he hides under a large bronze bell. Her intense emotions change her into a serpentlike demon, which encircles the bell. In the final scene, Anchin prays fervently for salvation, but the heat of Kiyohime's terrible rage melts the bell and incinerates both of them. In this netsuke, Kiyohime sits on top of the bell. She holds a mallet to strike the bell in one hand and pulls distractedly at her own hair with the other. The bell has a carved opening, which probably once revealed a figure of Anchin, now lost.

30

Yamauba and Kintarō, mid-18th century
Ivory with inlay; 4.8 cm
Unsigned

According to Japanese folklore, Kintarō, the child of the mountain witch Yamauba, lived in the forest and had animals for friends. Because of his extraordinary strength, Kintarō could even defeat bears in friendly wrestling matches. As a result, he came to the attention of the warlord Minamoto Yorimitsu (1056–1127), who made the boy a samurai after he helped to defeat a horde of demons. Artists usually portray Kintarō as a robust youth. This netsuke is unusual in its frank presentation of Kintarō as an infant with his mother. Yamauba, pictured with unkempt hair, bare breasts, and missing teeth, cries out as a crab pinches Kintarō's finger. The artist adroitly carved the composition from a triangular piece of raw ivory, a common practice with early netsuke makers.

31

Kan'u, early 18th century
Ivory; 12.5 cm
Unsigned

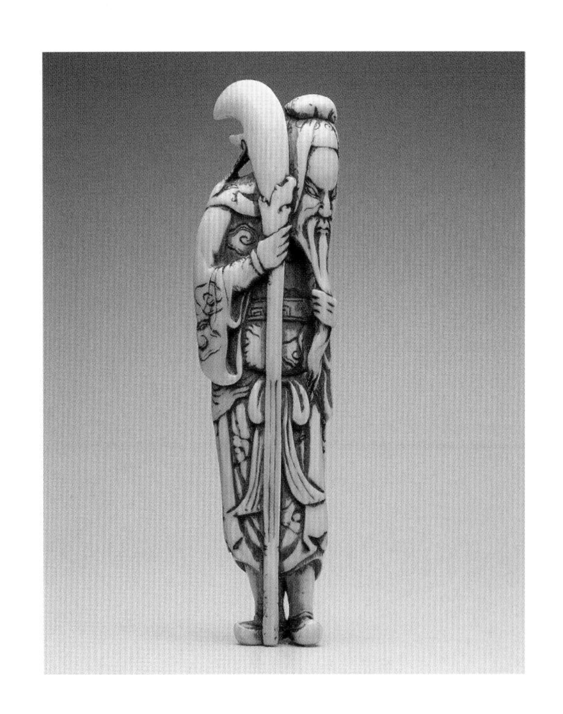

A legendary Chinese general whose exploits were chronicled in the *Romance of the Three Kingdoms*, Kan'u (Kuan Yu) was famous for his military prowess, noble character, and unwavering loyalty. As a result, the Chinese deified him as a god of war and a paragon of Confucian virtue. The Japanese became familiar with the Kan'u stories in the early 18th century, and there was even a Kabuki play about him performed in 1737 (Clark, *Ukiyo-e Paintings*, p. 104). As can be seen with this netsuke, Japanese artists typically portrayed Kan'u with a long beard and a stern expression, dressed in elaborate Chinese costume, and holding his halberd. The carving's triangular cross section, strongly delineated details, and "blank" eyes indicate its early date.

32

Kan'u on horseback, mid-18th century
Wood; 7.7 cm
Unsigned

This figure, while readily identifiable as Kan'u from the costume and halberd, is unusual in showing the general on horseback. Like other early netsuke carvers, the artist here was more concerned with creating a dynamic and elegant composition than in rendering the anatomical accuracy of the horse. Consequently, to produce a dramatic configuration, he bunched the animal's hooves together and made the steed's great neck twist backward, as if it is examining something on the ground behind it. Interestingly, the finished carving also imitates the triangular cross section of rough-cut ivory, although wood would not have had the same constraints.

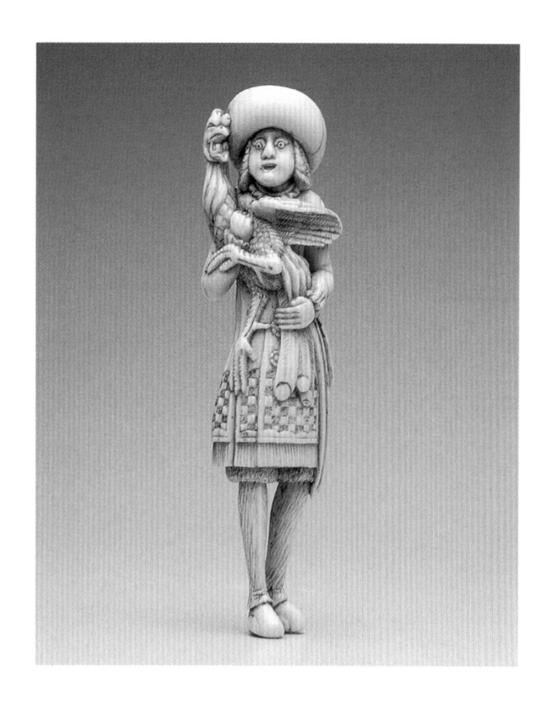

33

Dutchman and peacock, mid-18th century
Ivory; 11.5 cm
Unsigned

Portuguese traders first arrived in Japan in 1543, followed by the Spanish in 1592 and the Dutch in 1600. Under the Tokugawa government's 1638 policy of national isolationism, however, the Portuguese and Spanish were expelled and the Dutch restricted to the small island of Deshima, off the coast of Nagasaki. Early on, Japanese artists took great interest in these outsiders and pictured their tall ships and exotic clothing in folding screens and hanging scrolls. Netsuke artists, too, began carving images of the Europeans during the 18th century and probably were influenced by woodblock prints of the foreigners, which began to be published in the late 1740s and were called "Nagasaki *miyage*" (souvenirs of Nagasaki). In this netsuke, the unknown artist cleverly commented on the fancy clothes worn by the Dutch by pairing a young dandy with a peacock.

34

Dutch hunter, mid-18th century
Wood, horn, ivory, and coral; 11 cm
Unsigned

The bow and quiver of this tall figure indicate he is a hunter. The Japanese marveled at the stature of foreigners, and 18th-century carvers found them ideal subjects at a time when rather large netsuke were fashionable. The lapped coat, leggings, and long, curly hair of this work are typical of such images. The figure's fierce expression and the coat's swirling cloud pattern, however, are more commonly seen in representations of Taoist immortals, suggesting the unknown artist here was more familiar with Chinese themes rather than European ones. This might also account for the figure's curious lack of shoes. The ivory and black coral for the eyes and buttons predate the 19th century's more extensive use of inlay.

35

Fisherman with octopus, early 18th century
Wood; 12.2 cm
Signature undeciphered

This netsuke portrays a yawning fisherman with his catch. While artists sometimes portrayed octopuses as monsters, the creature here hangs benignly over the fisherman's shoulder. The man, however, seems frightening, with his emaciated chest, skeletal head, and gaping mouth.

36

Drummer, early 18th century
Plum wood and mica; 12 cm
Attributed to Miwa (Tokyo school)

This figure's curly, long hair and sarong suggest he is not Japanese but possibly a South Seas islander. Through limited exposure to Chinese and Dutch traders at the port of Nagasaki, the Japanese saw maps and drawings of people from faraway lands. This design might have been inspired by such books as the 1645 *Bankoku sōzu* (Complete Pictures of Various Lands) or the 1720 *Yonjūnikoku jimbutsu zusetsu* (Illustrated Account of the People of Forty-two Countries). The figure's eyes have been inlaid with mica, a technique associated with the earliest artist who used the name Miwa. The wear seen between the drummer's left arm and his body indicates the cord passed through that space. Curiously, however, a drilled opening can be found by the right elbow.

37

Dancing porter, mid-18th century
Wood; 10 cm
Unsigned

Artists often portrayed common laborers as happy-go-lucky buffoons because they were free from the social constraints and decorum that dictated the behavior of samurai and urban sophisticates. This practice can also be found in Kyōgen plays, wherein humor results from the outrageous antics of peasants who, nevertheless, often get the better of their learned masters. In this netsuke, the artist aptly captured the ungainly movements of a dancing porter, whose short robe has fallen open to reveal a sizable paunch.

38

Dancing fisherman, mid-18th century
Ivory with inlay; 8.8 cm
Unsigned

Like the previous example (cat. no. 37), this netsuke depicts a commoner dancing. The rhythm of the dance has been suggested by the figure's stamping foot and the tamborinelike instrument he uses to slap his thigh. The fisherman's partial nakedness and hairy body, however, suggest his uncouthness.

39

Bugaku dancer, early 18th century
Ivory; 7.8 cm
Unsigned

Netsuke artists delighted in presenting conventional subjects in novel ways. Here, a performer of Bugaku, an ancient court dance, has been portrayed relaxing, perhaps resting between performances. Humor arises from both its unusually informal treatment and its resemblance to miniature carvings of reclining nude women. Chinese and Japanese doctors used such figurines as a way of encouraging shy female patients to discreetly point to the location of their pain.

40

Baku, early 18th century
Ivory with horn inlay; 5.5 cm
Attributed to Gechu (Osaka school)

Mythical creatures, *baku* are usually portrayed with an elephant's tusks and long trunk and a lion's mane and body. Despite their crouched, menacing postures and scowling faces, *baku* are believed to be benevolent creatures that devour bad dreams. Thus, netsuke in their form acted as talismans against nightmares. The artist of this netsuke created a pleasing circular composition by having the *baku* twist backward to look behind itself. The creature's tapered head and trunk echo the mass of curls comprising its tail.

41

Kirin, mid-18th century
Painted cypress wood; 9.5 cm
Attributed to Yoshimura Shūzan (died 1776, Osaka school)

A composite beast from Chinese mythology, a *kirin* (*ch'i-lin* in Chinese) has a single horn (like a unicorn), a dragon's head, a deer's body, and a lion's tail. Sometimes, it is also depicted with scales. When a *kirin* appears, it brings good fortune, health, bountiful harvests, and widespread peace. Like other works attributed to Yoshimura Shūzan, this *kirin* was carved from cypress and then painted. According to Inaba Tsūryū, who published the first history about netsuke in 1781, Shūzan was a professional painter of the Kanō school, whose members specialized in Chinese themes. This netsuke, as was typical of Shūzan's works, is superbly dramatic: the beast's tortured posture is accentuated by the flames licking its body and the ball it loosely holds in its grimacing mouth.

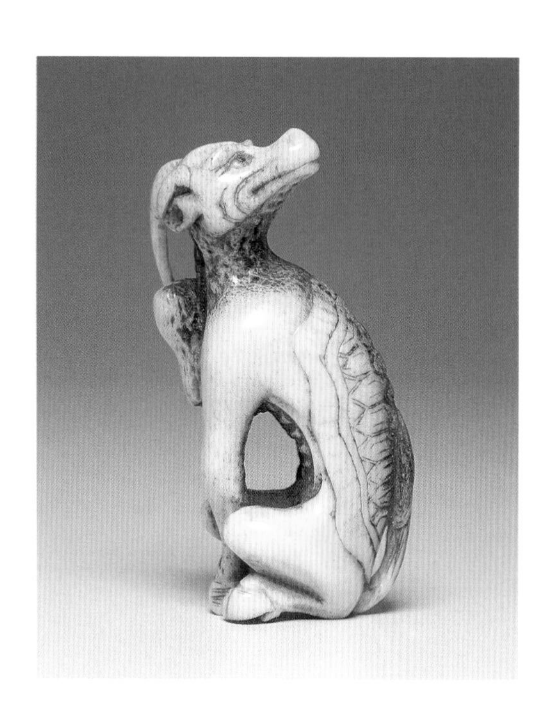

42

Seated *suisei*, early 18th century
Stag antler; 5.5 cm
Unsigned

Mythological creatures, *suisei* have goatlike bodies and tortoise carapaces. For this netsuke, the artist cleverly carved a piece of stag antler, using the natural grain of the material to create a distinctive stripe down the animal's back, neck, and underside. He also connected the *suisei*'s horn to its raised front leg, thus eliminating a sharp projection that might have snagged the fine fabric of the kimono or sash.

43

Shachihoko, mid-18th century

Wood with lacquer and horn; 7.3 cm

Unsigned

Imaginary fishlike creatures, *shachihoko* are associated with water and usually depicted with pig or tigerlike faces, spines, and tails held high above their backs. The Japanese often placed large bronze or clay *shachihoko* at the ridge beams of Buddhist halls, palaces, and castles to protect the structures from fire. The carver of this netsuke tucked the *shachihoko*'s tail under its body to create a more compact and functional design. The animal's small body makes the gaping mouth seem all the more ferocious. Using a technique known as *negoro*, the artist applied black lacquer over red lacquer and then lightly rubbed some away to suggest wear. Years of handling, however, have worn away both the black and red pigments, revealing the natural boxwood underneath.

During the 1780s, popular culture in Japan reached its zenith. The government, suffering from internal graft and corruption, rarely enforced its earlier repressive edicts. As a result, the "decadent" arts of the townspeople flourished. Netsuke production increased as well, becoming progressively refined in technique and witty in presentation to reflect the elegant tastes and easy savoir faire of *chōnin* sophisticates.

By the late 18th century, netsuke had become so much a part of fashionable male attire that Inaba Tsūryū devoted one volume of his *Sōken Kishō* (Appreciation of Superior Sword Furnishings), a seven-volume compendium about swords and related paraphernalia, to them. Published in 1781, the *Sōken Kishō* included biographical information about fifty-four netsuke artists with representative sketches of their carvings and brief comments.

Inaba's writings make clear that some netsuke artists had achieved such distinction that their works were being forged, while many others were still quite unknown. In some cases, Inaba himself knew little more than the carver's name. Nevertheless, the artists' diverse geographical locations indicate that by the third quarter of the 18th century netsuke production had become widespread in Japan. It was also immensely varied, with artists specializing in particular subjects and techniques.

While most of the craftsmen Inaba mentioned were his contemporaries, a few were famous sculptors or painters from the previous generation. Whether or not these earlier men actually made netsuke remains unverifiable, but Inaba might have been trying to establish a respectable lineage for his generation of netsuke artists. Indeed, his book suggests that carving netsuke was becoming a viable profession in its own right, as does the fact that artists began to regularly sign their works during the final decades of the 18th century. In fact, the founders of many of the netsuke schools that flourished during the early 19th century were active during Inaba's time. They included the Tokyo artists Miwa, Shūgetsu, Minkoku, Gessen, and Shibayama; the Kyoto artists Okatomo, Yoshinaga, Tomotada, Yoshitomo, and Mitsuhide; the Osaka artists Sanko and Tsuji; and the Tsu (Ise province) artists Minkō and Kōkei.

While netsuke artists continued to craft tall figures into the 19th century, they increasingly made smaller, more compact compositions. It has been suggested that stringent government restrictions on ostentatious displays might have led to this reduction in scale, thus allowing *chōnin* to lavish great sums on these jewellike treasures while appearing to be appropriately discreet and modest (Brown, "Why Art Historians Don't Study Netsuke," p. 15). In fact, the carving of tall figures continued well past the Kyōhō Reforms of the 1720s, which aimed at reducing the indebtedness of the samurai class, exhorted all citizens to lead more frugal lives, and included restrictions against extravagant dress.

Ironically, the popularity of smaller netsuke began to appear from 1760 to 1786 during the relatively lax reign of the shogun Ieharu and his corrupt minister Tanuma Okitsugu. It seems likely, therefore, that miniaturization itself became an admired characteristic, with artists vying to achieve novel surface effects and details that would astound their most demanding customers.

At the same time, carvers began to use a greater variety of materials and to embellish their netsuke with contrasting inlays of horn, shell, coral, and stone to suggest such minutiae as the pupils of eyes. They also lavished great care on every aspect of their netsuke; some even lined the *himotoshi* with finely fashioned bits of ivory.

Miniaturization itself became an admired characteristic, with artists vying to achieve novel surface effects and details that would astound their most demanding customers.

Netsuke artists also started to draw their subjects from Japan's own rich history and mythology. For instance, they transformed legendary warriors, like the 12th-century samurai Minamoto Yorimasa and his faithful retainer Ii-no-Hayata (cat. no. 62), into premodern action figures. They also depicted tragic heros from famous Nō and Kabuki plays. Minkō, for instance, created a number of netsuke representing the tragically obsessed heroine Kiyohime (from the Nō play *Dojoji*) pursuing the object of her misplaced affections, the hapless monk Anchin (cat. no. 61). And they increasingly drew inspiration from the world around them by carving samurai (cat. no. 66), sumō wrestlers (cat. no. 71), aristocratic football players (cat. no. 65), and even lowly fishermen (cat. no. 70).

During the late 18th century, the stylized distortions that had characterized earlier netsuke began to be replaced by a new naturalism. This trend first appeared in other art forms, notably in the paintings of Maruyama Ōkyo (1733–95) and his followers. To a large degree, this phenomenon can be attributed to the repeal of the ban on imported books, which was part of the earlier Kyōhō Reforms of 1722. Chinese manuals on herbal pharmacology, for example, illustrated botanical specimens in scientific detail, and Dutch engravings showed anatomical studies of humans and animals using Western chiaroscuro and foreshortening.

Inspired by these renderings, Maruyama school painters skillfully adopted European techniques to imbue their subjects with a greater sense of volume and anatomical accuracy than had ever been seen before in Japan. This new approach, carefully combined with elements of native decorative design, became an immediate sensation, and Maruyama artists and Shijō school painters began to rival members of the established Kano ateliers.

Following this lead, netsuke artists began to produce works of astonishing realism as well. Minkoku starkly portrayed the famous 9th-century poet Ono-no-Komachi in her old age, carefully carving her bent back, withered breasts, sunken cheeks, and gaping mouth (cat. no. 64). Using the same accuracy to depict animals, Kōkei convincingly rendered the bony angularity and rippling musculature of an ox (cat. no. 82) and inlaid bits of polished horn to simulate the beast's shiny eyes. This attention to naturalistic detail even lent a degree of believability to depictions of imaginary creatures. The Kyoto artist Yoshitomo, for example, created a plausible nine-tailed fox (cat. no. 78) by correctly rendering its anatomy, while hyperextending its posture to suggest supernatural flight. Yoshitomo's choice of ivory, too, appropriately conveyed the belief that the fur of especially old and potent foxes turns white.

Earthy humor also began to appear in late 18th-century netsuke, reflecting the playful, somewhat ribald nature of *chōnin* culture. At times, artists would imbue their netsuke with a subtle humor by cleverly varying established themes. For instance, they traditionally showed the gods of wind and thunder charging wrathfully across the skies. But Shunsai portrayed the wind god cinching his bag of wind, while gently creating a breeze with a fan (cat. no. 55). Likewise, Kazuhide's depiction of the fertility goddess Okame as a lustful rat catcher (cat. no. 59) attains humor because of its lewd irreverence. Sometimes, netsuke artists also used humor as social commentary. Minkō, for example, represented a sake seller as a demon (cat. no. 52) to suggest the dangerously tempting nature of that profession. It should not be supposed, however, that the owner of such a netsuke seriously objected to liquor. More likely, he feigned damnation of the sake trade while gleefully drinking a toast to the vendor's prompt delivery.

44

Chinnan, late 18th century
Ivory; 9 cm
Unsigned

Usually, the Taoist immortal Chinnan (Ch'en-nan) holds a begging bowl, from which he summons the rain dragon (see cat. no. 9). In this netsuke, however, he has a jewel, the dragon's traditional attribute. The beast has climbed onto his shoulders and seems to be struggling for a foothold, while the sage is in mid-step. Although it resembles earlier netsuke of standing Taoist immortals, the work has several elements that became prevalent during the late 18th century, including the refined carving, the precisely reticulated flames around the dragon, and the inventive positioning of the *himotoshi* between the dragon and the back of the sage's neck. The odd positioning of Chinnan's feet, however, as well as the reversed order of his right toes, seems curious given the expert carving of the piece but adds to its overall strangeness.

45

Ikkaku, late 18th century
Ivory; 7.5 cm
Attributed to Sanko (Osaka school)

The Taoist immortal Ikkaku lost his magical powers because of his all-too-human infatuation with a beautiful woman (see cat. no. 11). Like other netsuke of the immortal, the carving here shows Ikkaku carrying his temptress on his back. Aware of her effect on the sage, the young woman coquettishly covers her smile in mock modesty. Although unsigned, the netsuke closely resembles the few remaining works by Sanko, an Osaka artist mentioned in Inaba Tsūryū's *Sōken Kishō* of 1781. Deep undercutting, crisp details, and fluttering draperies enliven the composition, while the naturalistic proportions of the figures distinguish the netsuke from earlier, elongated renderings of the subject.

46

Kanzan and Jittoku, late 18th century

Ivory; 6.3 cm

Signed: *Yoshinaga* (Kyoto school)

The 7th-century Chinese poet Kanzan (Han-shan) and his companion, the orphan Jittoku (Shih-te), have long been admired by Zen Buddhists for their pure, unfettered lifestyle (see cat. no. 17). This netsuke portrays Jittoku leaning on the brushwood broom he uses to sweep the kitchen floor, while the pair laughs over a scroll of Kanzan's poetry. The precisely carved surface, seen in the minute details of the figures' costumes, their hair, and Jittoku's straw skirt, attests to the skill of the Kyoto artist Yoshinaga. Although little is known about him, his period of activity was established in Inaba Tsūryū's *Sōken Kishō* as the late 18th century.

47

Seiōbo with basket, late 18th century

Wood; 8 cm

Unsigned

In Taoism, Seiōbo (Hsi-wang-mu), or Queen Mother of the West, is a mythical fairy goddess who lives in China's Kunlun Mountains. Legend says that peaches of immortality grow in her splendid gardens. An imperial adviser, lusting after everlasting life, once stole some of the magical fruit (see cat. nos. 14 and 15). Chinese painters often depict Seiōbo as an elegant aristocrat descending from the clouds on the back of a phoenix. In this netsuke, the ethereal woman carries a woven basket holding one of her magical peaches.

48

***Niō* guardian**, late 18th century
Wood; 6.5 cm
Signed: *Gessen* (Tokyo school)

Niō, literally "two kings," are fierce Buddhist guardians. Large sculptural images of the two figures usually flank the entrances to Japanese temples and portray them as tense and muscular with clenched fists and menacing postures. Artists further suggested their divine fury by showing their robes and scarves blowing about them, as if caught in a maelstrom. Clearly influenced by the monumental sculpture he saw on temple visits, the netsuke artist Gessen rendered the miniature guardian here in remarkable detail, down to his knuckles and fingernails.

49

Recumbent *Niō* guardian, late 18th century
Marine ivory; 6.8 cm
Unsigned

The tendency to humanize religious and historic figures became a popular trend during the Edo period and reflected the playful, somewhat irreverent attitudes of the rising middle class. This amusing netsuke shows a *Niō* guardian lying down, as if taking a break, and gently cradling his head in his hand. The figure's posture and partial nakedness also resemble the miniature carvings of nude women that Chinese and Japanese doctors used with their shy female patients to point to the location of their pain. Thus, the humor here is compounded by the artist's mildly impious substitution of a *Niō* for a woman.

50

Seated demon, late 18th century
Ivory with horn inlay; 7.8 cm
Unsigned

Artists have long delighted in showing demons getting the better of Shōki (Chung K'uei), a T'ang scholar who vowed to rid the world of evil for all eternity (see cat. no. 1). In this netsuke, a demon smiles innocently while casually lounging. His naughty antics become evident, however, when the netsuke is turned over. For beneath him, he hides Shōki's sword. The imp's twisted torso and unnaturally jutting right shoulder suggest that the carver adapted his design to make the most of a triangular section of ivory. This characteristic, together with the overall boldness of the carving, recalls earlier works, but the inlaid eyes and lively, caricaturelike quality of the face suggest a late 18th-century date.

51

Demon and ghost on a lotus leaf, late 18th century
Wood with inlay; 5 cm
Unsigned

According to the Buddhist concept of death and the transmigration of the soul, those who cannot achieve salvation are reborn in one of six realms. The lowest realm consists of a variety of hells. There, grotesque *oni*, or demons, torture the condemned by various means. As early as the 12th century, Japanese artists painted graphic scenes of hell, showing the sinners as naked emaciated figures dwarfed by their *oni* keepers. Such images reminded people of the dire fate that awaited them if they were impious and committed evil deeds. Something of the Edo period's light-heartedness, however, is evident in this netsuke, which depicts a sinner and an *oni* more like cohorts, with the sinner giving the *oni* a back-rub. Both rest on a lotus leaf, a plant symbolic of Buddhist purity.

52

Demon with sake bucket, late 18th century
Wood; 7 cm
Signed: *Gose Minkō* (Tanaka Minkō, 1735–1816, Tsu school)

Oni are horned, fanged, ferocious demons. As servants to the King of Hell, they carry out grisly punishments against sinners. *Oni* also personify evil and are often shown enacting some sort of mischief. In this work, a smiling *oni* symbolizes temptation itself, as he apes the actions of a sake vendor. He carries a cask of the strong rice wine in one hand and a delivery list in the other. This is an unusual subject for the Tsu artist Minkō, who is better known for his chubby and amusing animals.

53

Demon mask, late 18th century
Wood with horn inlay; 4.8 cm
Signature undeciphered

This comical mask of an *oni*, or demon, seems more like a children's mask instead of the sinister visages often encountered in Nō theatricals. It might, in fact, have been inspired by the playful masks worn by men during *setsubun* rituals, when children throw beans at "demons" to rid their houses of evil. The humorousness of this netsuke is heightened by the demon's round head, large eyes, and fangs, which grow in opposite directions.

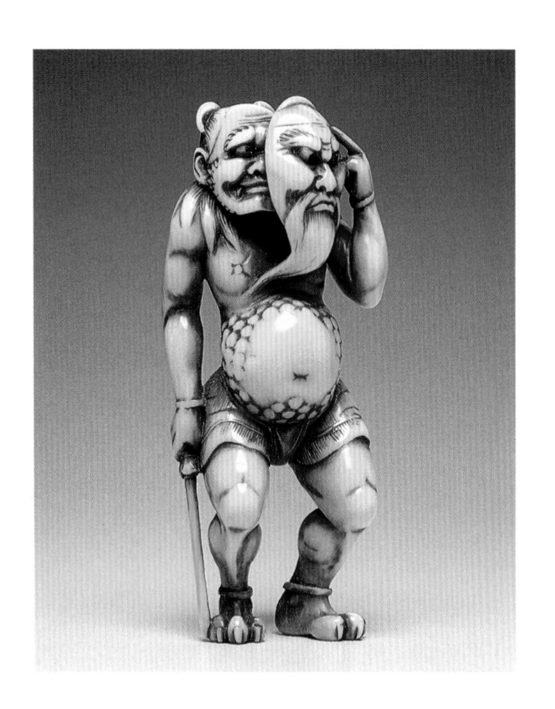

54

Demon with a mask of Shōki, late 18th century
Ivory with inlay; 9 cm
Unsigned

Shōki (Chung K'uei) was a 7th-century Chinese scholar who vowed to rid the world of evil (see cat. no. 1). Despite Shōki's noble promise, Chinese and Japanese artists often showed the "demon queller" being bested by various mischievous imps. In this netsuke, a demon wears a mask of Shōki and holds his sword, perhaps to amuse his fellow fiends. The artist might also have been cleverly pointing out the duplicitous nature of many self-righteous people, who wear "masks" of piety to conceal their own foibles. Regardless, the artist of this large and impressive netsuke gave his supernatural subject new realism through the figure's convincing musculature, solid stance, and reptilian skin (seen around the belly and the backs of the thighs).

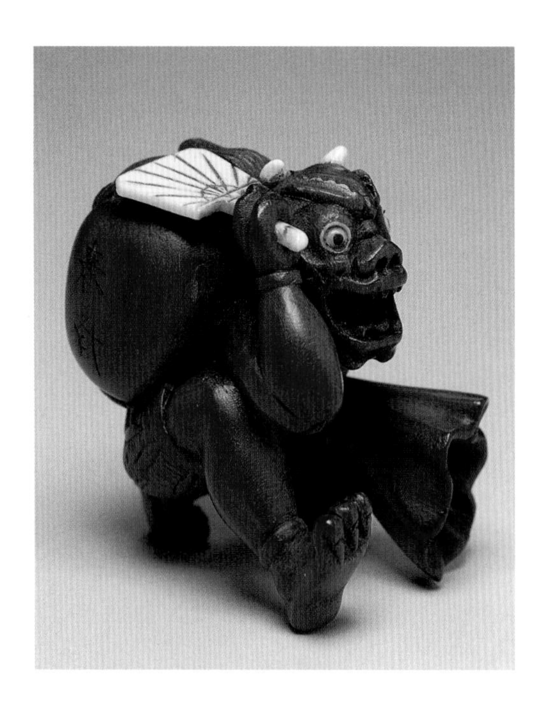

55

God of wind, late 18th century
Wood with ivory and coral; 4 cm
Signed: *Shunsai* (school unknown)

This humorous netsuke shows the god of wind (*Fūjin)* using a fan to make a gentle breeze. Meanwhile, he cinches the neck of his bag to contain the wind. The imprisoned maelstrom makes the sack bulge and press against his back, causing him to dig in his right heel for balance. The restrained use of inlaid materials as embellishments typifies netsuke from the late 18th century. The perfectly round ivory eyes with coral pupils are especially effective, giving the god a comically wild, wide-eyed appearance.

56

Fukurokuju, late 18th century

Wood; 4.3 cm

Signed: *Tsuji* (Osaka school)

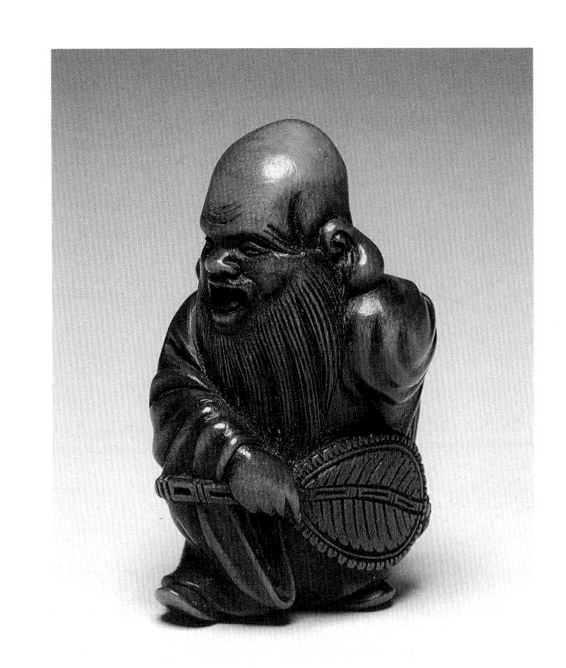

Fukurokuju is one of the Seven Gods of Good Fortune (*shichi fukujin*), a group of deities adopted into Japanese worship from China as early as the 15th century. Fukurokuju's distinguishing feature is an elongated cranium, probably suggesting the vast wisdom he accumulated over his long life. In the *Sōken Kishō,* Inaba Tsūryū mentions that Tsuji, the maker of this netsuke, was a skilled carver who never used ivory, an unusual circumstance for an 18th-century artist working in a major city where ivory predominated. Tsuji's compositions also tended to be compact, presaging the 19th-century penchant for smaller netsuke. And despite the fantastic nature of his subjects, Tsuji carved them with a greater naturalism than had been achieved earlier. (Fukurokuju's robe, for example, falls in soft, fluid folds.) Moreover, Tsuji must have been particularly fond of this composition, for he sculpted it several times with only slight variations.

57

Hotei on ox, late 18th century

Wood; 7.8 cm

Unsigned

This netsuke shows the Zen Buddhist monk Hotei (Pu-tai) riding an ox, an iconography usually reserved for Roshi (Lao-tzu), the legendary founder of Taoism who left China on an ox after writing the *Tao Te Ching* in the 6th century B.C. The unusual juxtaposition here, however, might not have been arbitrary. In Zen literature, the progressively harmonious relationship between a young herder and his ox symbolizes the quest for spiritual enlightenment. In addition, the *Ten Ox Herding Songs,* poems about each successive stage, became popular with Chinese monks during the Southern Sung Dynasty (1127–1279) and well known in Japan by the 15th century. Portraying the happy wanderer Hotei, then, in the guise of an enlightened herder seems not only appropriate but inspired. Moreover, the intellectual sophistication of this piece is matched by its skillful execution. The top of Hotei's head and the ox's bunched hooves both taper to form the ends of the composition. An artful contrast also exists between the spare rendering of Hotei's smooth, fleshy body and simple robes and the extensive incising of the ox's fur.

58

Hotei with children, late 18th century
Wood; 5.3 cm
Unsigned

Zen painters often pictured the eccentric Buddhist priest Hotei (Pu-tai) as a happy wanderer unconcerned with material wealth. Ironically, artists later made Hotei into one of their gods of good fortune, and the traveler's sack he carried was said to contain treasure. In this netsuke, he opens his bag to reveal true wealth—joyous children. The unknown artist of this delightfully original composition showed Hotei playfully trying to contain three rambunctious boys in his sack by pulling the fabric up with his hands. When this is not enough, he resorts to using his teeth.

59

Okame with rat and cat, late 18th century
Ivory; 5 cm
Signed: *Kazuhide* (school unknown)

According to the earliest histories of Japan, the sun goddess once sequestered herself in a cave, plunging the world into darkness. In turn, the female deity Ama-no-Uzame performed a lively dance outside the cave to lure her out. Ama-no-Uzame later became popularized as Okame, a goddess of fertility, abundance, and mirth. As such, she is portrayed as a happy country girl of prodigious girth and insatiable sexual appetite. In comic Kyōgen plays, she lustfully pursues unwilling lovers. In other depictions, she carries a gigantic *matsutake* mushroom or tugs on a mountain goblin's long nose, both obvious phallic references. In netsuke, she is sometimes shown gratifying herself by thrusting a rat between her legs. Here, her lustful plan has failed. Her own cat has been caught in the trap while the rat scampers away.

60

Ashinaga and Tenaga, late 18th century
Wood; 12.4 cm
Unsigned

According to Chinese mythology, strange people live along the Eastern Sea. Long-legged men (Ashinaga) carry their long-armed brothers (Tenaga) on their shoulders into the ocean, where they snatch fish from the deep water. When pictured together, the two races stand for the benefits of peaceful coexistence. Despite the fanciful nature of the subject, this netsuke achieves a degree of realism by each figure's individualization. Ashinaga has a potbelly, square jaw, and broad, happy face; Tenaga, a thin, bearded face and somewhat pensive expression. Close inspection reveals that Tenaga once held something in his left hand, possibly a fish or clam, but damage or wear has caused that detail to be lost.

61

Kiyohime and Anchin, late 18th century
Ebony, ivory, and brass; 5.3 cm
Signed: *Minkō* (Tanaka Minkō, 1735–1816, Tsu school)

In the popular Nō play *Dojoji*, a young woman's intense passion for a monk transforms her into a serpentlike demon (see cat. no. 29). The artist here, Minkō, was one of the first to create "trick" netsuke. Twisting the top of this piece makes Anchin's face, white with fear, appear in an opening near the demonlike Kiyohime. With an additional turn, his face becomes red from the heat of Kiyohime's wrath. With a final twist, his face becomes bluish black, suggesting his death. Minkō carved the work in his typically bold style and included several extra touches, like the flame red tongue, brass inlaid eyes, and ivory-lined cord openings (*himotoshi*).

62

Slaying the *nue*, late 18th century
Boxwood and brass; 4.8 cm
Signed: *Minkō* (Tanaka Minkō, 1735–1816, Tsu school)

The Japanese often credit their most illustrious warriors with fantastic exploits. One legend about the famous 12th-century leader Minamoto Yorimasa describes his battle with a *nue*, a beast with the head of a monkey, the claws of a tiger, and the tail of a snake. The story tells of a *nue* that was haunting the imperial palace, causing the emperor to become ill. After lying-in-wait, Yorimasa shoots the *nue* with an arrow. His retainer, Ii-no-Hayata, then finishes it off with his sword, as seen in this netsuke. The figures here have hefty physiques, a common practice for Minkō who liked his personages comically plump. The large, orblike eyes with inlaid brass also typify his style.

63

Kan'u, late 18th century
Wood with lacquer and colored ivory; 7.7 cm
Signed: *Minkoku* (Tokyo school)

A legendary Chinese general, Kan'u (Kuan Yu) was revered in both China and Japan not only as a god of war but as a paragon of Confucian virtue (see cat. nos. 31 and 32). Like other representations of the stalwart general, the figure here is in elaborate military garb and shown grasping his halberd. The great finesse of this rendering, however, clearly distinguishes it as Minkoku's handiwork. He covered the general's robes with minute patterns that suggest sumptuous Chinese brocades. He also carved the wide belt with a meandering geometric pattern and included a demon's-head clasp with interlocking rings and animal-hair tassels. Despite this astonishing level of detail, Minkoku kept the overall composition simple, masterfully conveying Kan'u's dignity and implacability through the stability of his pose.

64

Ono-no-Komachi, late 18th century
Wood; 7.4 cm
Signed: *Minkoku* (Tokyo school)

Ono-no-Komachi (834–80) was one of the "Six Great Poets" of 9th-century Japan. Extremely beautiful as a young woman, she cruelly rejected all suitors and is said to have passed her old age in solitude and squalor. Because of this, she came to symbolize *mono-no-aware*, the melancholy awareness that all enjoyment is fleeting and thus tinged with sadness. Artists frequently showed her as old and decrepit. Here, Minkoku portrayed her leaning heavily on a walking stick and carrying all her earthly belongings in a patchwork sack and basket. Her hat is tattered and her robe falls open, revealing her emaciated chest and withered breasts. Minkoku's skill at depicting the human form is best seen in Komachi's pitiful face, with its sunken cheeks, rheumy eyes, and gaping mouth with one lone tooth.

65

***Kemari* player**, late 18th century
Lacquered wood with traces of silver and gold; 9.2 cm
Unsigned

A Chinese game introduced to Japan, *kemari* involves eight players who try to keep a deerskin ball aloft by kicking it to one another. Traditionally played by noblemen, *kemari* was enjoyed by all classes of Japanese society during the Edo period. This figure of a Chinese court official suggests the game's origins. The artist further imbued the work with a Chinese "flavor" by using *negoro*, a lacquer technique from mainland China. He applied red lacquer over black and then rubbed some away to suggest the wear that occurs from years of handling.

66

Rōnin, late 18th century
Wood; 4.6 cm
Signed: *Minkō* (Tanaka Minkō, 1735–1816, Tsu school)

A *rōnin* (literally, "a person tossed about on the waves") is a samurai who has lost his master. During the 17th century, such disenfranchised warriors became a problematical subclass in Japan. Wandering the countryside, they often engaged in mercenary activities, thus forsaking their samurai code of ethics. In this netsuke, a menacing *rōnin* crouches while grasping the hilt of his sword. Befitting his reduced circumstances, he wears the simple woven hat and straw raincoat of a commoner.

67

Dutchman with small figure, late 18th century
Wood; 10 cm
Unsigned

This netsuke reflects the Japanese fascination with the Dutch, made all the more mysterious by the government restricting them to the small island of Deshima and forbidding contact with the Japanese, except for official representatives (see cat. no. 33). The artist here carefully rendered the Dutch trader's pronounced facial features, as well as his long coat with its tasseled hem, his shoes, and his cap. The inclusion of the curiously small figure squatting on the Dutchman's right shoe and clinging to his coat might have also had added meaning. Some woodblock print artists pictured such "little people" in their designs—Lilliputians who spied on full-sized people and humorously commented on their actions.

68

Dutchman holding a puppy, late 18th century
Wood with inlay; 9.3 cm
Signed: *Jobun* (Tokyo school)

The Tokyo artist Jobun made several netsuke of foreigners with their exotic small dogs. Here, he humorously integrated a natural knot in the wood to suggest the dog had an "accident" on the European's topcoat. The Dutchman holds his hand to his head, exasperated by his bad luck. Jobun increased the comic aspect of pieces like this by carving them from long, slender sections of wood to exaggerate the tallness of these outlandish strangers. This particular design must have become extremely popular, for later Japanese artists produced many similar images.

69

Fox and hunter, late 18th century
Stag antler; 8 cm
Unsigned

The Japanese believe foxes capable of changing themselves into human form to beguile the unsuspecting. In the popular Kyōgen play *Tsurigitsune*, an old fox changes into a priest to escape being hunted. He reminds the hunter about the Buddhist commandments against taking life and eating meat, and the ruse seems to work. On the way home, however, the priest encounters a baited trap and cannot resist the enticing smell of roasted rat. He transforms back into a fox, takes the food, and is caught. In this imaginative netsuke, the fox and hunter occupy opposite sides of the same work. The hunter kneels as if lying-in-wait for the fox, his head covered by a rush mat. The fox wears the robes and hood of a priest and leans heavily on a staff. The artist has cleverly adapted his design to the confines of the stag antler.

70

Fisherman with conch, late 18th century
Wood; 14 cm
Unsigned

According to Chinese legend, mermaids hold conch shells to their ears to hear the secrets of the ocean. In this comical netsuke, a lowly fisherman gasps in surprise as he listens to the sea's mysterious voice. Curiously, this figure has an unusual feature—the loose ball in his mouth. Netsuke artists frequently showed dragons and *shishi* with cosmic pearls in their mouths, but no iconographical precedent exists for its inclusion here. Possibly, the artist simply wanted to demonstrate the scope of his carving abilities. But the ball, the reticulated portions of the grass skirt, and the way the arms and legs extend free from the original block of wood all suggest a high level of skill and a late 18th-century date. The uniformity of the *himotoshi* also indicates the piece was made in the late 1700s.

71

Sumō wrestler, late 18th century
Ivory with inlay; 9 cm
Unsigned

The robust proportions and strong arms of this man identify him as a sumō wrestler. The artist carved the figure from the outer portion of an ivory tusk, as indicated by the slight convexity of the wrestler's back. The outer rind also aged differently from the inner rind, turning orange over time. While the size and boldness of the piece recall early 18th-century works, the inlaid eyes and subtle surface finish suggest a later date. The subject matter, too, reflects the growing interest netsuke carvers had in genre themes during the second half of the 18th century.

72

Chinese child with goat, late 18th century
Ivory with horn inlay; 6.5 cm
Unsigned (Kyoto school)

The Chinese painted images of robust male children to signify fecundity. Pictures of one-hundred children at play, in fact, became standard on embroidered textiles and lacquerware given to newlyweds and were a wish for speedy and frequent procreation. Japanese artists also used the theme of Chinese children (*karako*) for the same reason. Such children are easily recognizable by their costumes, shaved heads, and paired topknots. Because this netsuke shows a happy Chinese boy cradling a long-haired goat, it might have been commissioned to commemorate the Asian year of the goat.

73

Islander with telescope, late 18th century
Wood; 6.3 cm
Signed: *Gessen* (Tokyo school)

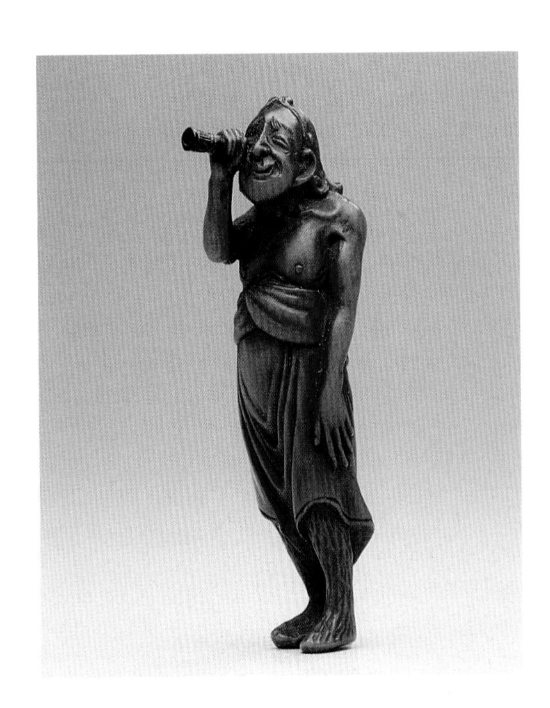

The Tokyo artists Gessen and Gessho made numerous netsuke showing South Seas islanders (discernible by their long, curly hair and sarongs) testing eggs for embryo development by holding them up to sunlight. This figure has a telescope, possibly a modification of that earlier theme. Gessen might also have derived this unusual subject from such books as the 1645 *Bankoku sōzu* (Complete Pictures of Various Lands) or the 1720 *Yonjūnikoku jimbutsu zusetsu* (Illustrated Account of the People of Forty-two Countries), which showed diverse people clothed in their native costumes and holding exotic implements.

74

Baku, late 18th century
Ivory with inlay; 4.6 cm
Unsigned (Kyoto school)

A *baku* has a lion's body and mane, a unicorn's single horn, and an elephant's long snout and tusks. The Japanese believed that *baku* aided humans by devouring their nightmares, and netsuke artists delighted in rendering these fantastic creatures in playful, imaginative ways. This miniature has the bold carving and warm, stained surface of ivory netsuke made in Kyoto. The animal's distinctive posture, as it crouches and turns to look behind itself, also typifies works by Kyoto artists.

75

***Baku* and young**, late 18th century
Ivory; 4 cm
Unsigned

In the popular Nō play *Shakkyō* (Stone Bridge), two *shishi* play with a magical jewel while guarding the famous natural bridge of Mount T'ien-t'ai in southeastern China. The creatures' powerful, earthshaking dance is said to dispel all evil. In an interesting variation on that theme, this netsuke shows a *baku* and its young cavorting with a round jewel, or ball. They appear both exotic and ridiculous, engulfed by luxurious curls and sporting tightly coiled trunks. Like catalogue number 74, this netsuke probably was carved by a Kyoto artist, but its fantastic presentation makes it refreshingly original.

76

Dragon, late 18th century
Ivory and coral; 2.7 cm
Unsigned

Unlike Westerners who see dragons as evil, fire-breathing beasts who prey on humans, Asians traditionally associate dragons with water and life-giving rains. For Buddhists, a dragon cavorting in clouds symbolizes the soaring, enlightened spirit and is often shown with a wish-granting jewel. This netsuke depicts a tightly coiled dragon sitting in a half-sphere, which resembles an oversized jewel. The creature's supernatural nature has been indicated by flames, which have been deeply carved and, in some areas, fully reticulated. The underside of the sphere is hollow, suggesting the netsuke might have also been used as an ash receptacle.

77

Dragon arising from a begging bowl, late 18th century
Ivory; 6.3 cm
Attributed to Tomotada (Kyoto school)

Netsuke artists commonly represented the Taoist immortal Chinnan (Ch'en-nan) summoning a rain dragon from his begging bowl (see cat. nos. 9 and 10). In this piece, however, we only see Chinnan's bowl, from which a dragon emerges amid curling wisps of smoke and supernatural flames. While several Kyoto artists used this design, the boldness of the carving here strongly suggests the hand of Tomotada.

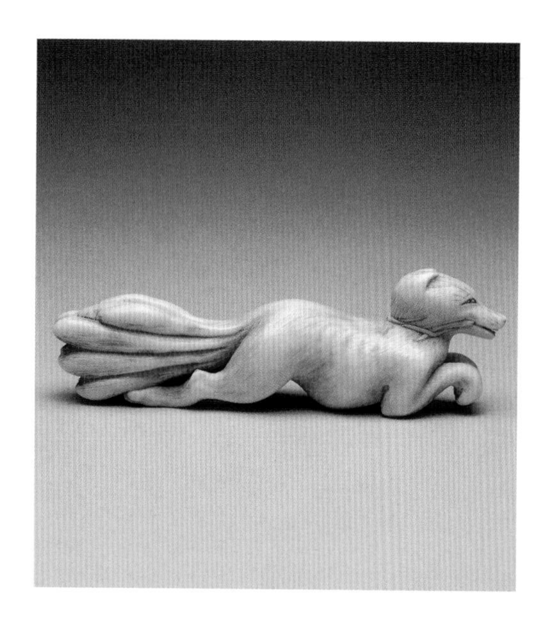

78

Nine-tailed fox, late 18th century
Ivory; 8.5 cm
Signed: *Yoshitomo* (Kyoto school)

The Japanese believe foxes possess supernatural powers, including the ability to change themselves into human form. A fox with white fur and nine tails was considered especially potent, having lived for hundreds of years. Generally, the occurrence of such a fox was thought to be lucky, but not always. The 12th-century emperor Toba, for example, is said to have been obsessed with one of his concubines. He soon fell ill and became dangerously weak. A court physician, suspecting the woman to be a malicious fox, staged a Buddhist ceremony where she would have to give prayers for her ailing lord. Before the startled eyes of the other courtiers, she changed back into a nine-tailed fox and fled the palace. The white fox here, however, holds a sheath of rice in his mouth, suggesting he is the messenger of Inari, the Japanese god of agriculture. As such, this netsuke would have functioned as an auspicious talisman.

79

Mythical lion (*shishi*) with hatchling, late 18th century
Ivory; 6.3 cm
Unsigned (Kyoto school)

In both Chinese and Japanese art, a lion is often paired with a dragon, with the lion symbolizing earth and the dragon, heaven. Like dragons, lions are often shown cavorting with flaming heavenly jewels. When depicted in pairs, a male lion holds the jewel, while a slightly smaller female shelters a cub under her paw. This netsuke humorously plays on that idea, with a cub hatching from the jewel. Such playfulness, also seen in the mother's outrageously curling tail, distinguishes this netsuke from earlier examples of the same subject.

80

Mythical lion (*shishi*) with ball (or jewel), late 18th century
Wood; 6 cm
Unsigned

This powerful carving might have been inspired by the monumental sculptures of *shishi* found throughout Japan and China. The artist here, however, deviated from tradition by endowing this *shishi*, which are usually male, with female genitalia. In this way, he subtly commented on the strength and dignity of women.

81

Ningyo, late 18th century
Stag antler; 12 cm
Unsigned

Not surprisingly, Japan, as a country heavily dependent on the ocean and its bounty, developed a rich mythology about sea creatures. But while the concept of *ningyo* (literally, "human-fish") exists in Japan, such creatures were not as prominent for the Japanese as the aquatic sirens of Western lore. And although many netsuke artists depicted *ningyo*, they are not as common as other themes. When they were represented, however, they usually appear as bare-breasted women with the flaring tails of fish. This netsuke is unusual in that the creature's sex is not readily discernible because platelike scales cover the upper torso where breasts normally would have been. Moreover, the artist made his subject even more exotic by giving it the heavy facial features and curly locks normally seen in depictions of foreigners.

82

Ox, late 18th century
Wood with horn inlay; 5.8 cm
Signed: *Kōkei* (Tsu school)

A student of the noted carver Minkō, Kōkei carried on the naturalistic style he championed. In this netsuke, Kōkei skillfully captured the angularity of the ox's underlying skeleton and powerful musculature. But instead of minutely incising the animal's fur, as Minkō would have done, Kōkei polished the surface smooth to convey the sheen of stiff ox hair. And rather than using brass for the eyes, as was typical of Minkō's inlays, he carved around the eyeballs, leaving them raised and using only a bit of horn for the pupils.

83

Cow and calf, late 18th century
Ebony; 7 cm
Signed: *Soun* (school unknown)

Little is known about the netsuke maker Soun. But for this work, he probably was influenced by the Kyoto artist Tomotada, who achieved fame for his carvings of oxen. The pronounced eye sockets, double halter, and long twisted rope seen here, which has been finely carved in relief and snakes over the animal's great mass, are all characteristics of Tomotada's cattle. Nevertheless, Soun gave his piece an appealing sense of movement and warmth by having the calf gently lick the cow's muzzle. Despite the naturalistic style of both artists, however, they took great care to make their netsuke completely functional and without any sharp projections. They placed the cattle's hooves, for instance, close to the animals' bodies and curved their horns downward, next to their faces. That detail, in fact, acknowledged a common Japanese practice: herders routinely weighted down the horns of their oxen, forcing them to grow in such a way to prevent the animals from goring one another.

84

Hare, late 18th century
Ivory with carnelian inlay; 5.4 cm
Signed: *Yoshinaga* (Kyoto school)

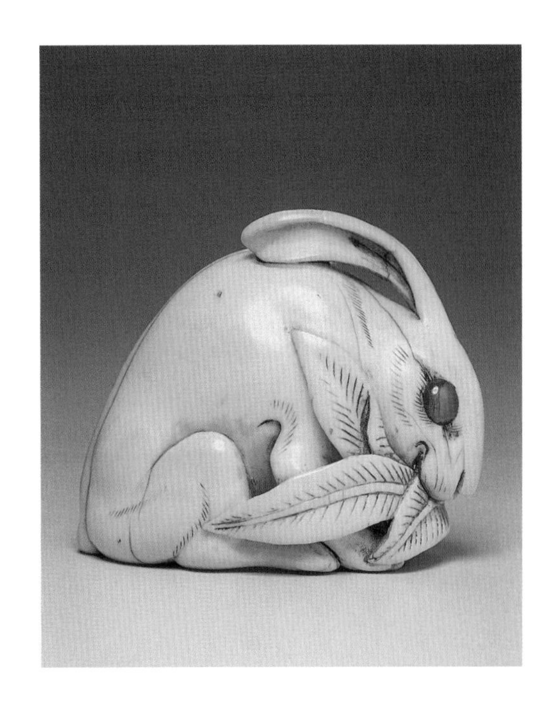

Yoshinaga, Masanao, Tomotada, and Okatomo are the earliest known artists to have worked in Kyoto. In many ways, however, Yoshinaga's carvings proved transitional, reflecting his increasing interest in naturalism and Japanese subjects, which foreshadowed the 19th-century's fascination with flora and fauna. However, the way Yoshinaga fashioned this hare—with bent ears, weak hindquarters, and artificially arranged leaves to create a dramatic, semicircular composition—typifies 18th-century designs. The fourth animal of the Asian zodiac, this rabbit may also represent the cosmic lunar hare, which produces the elixir of immortality by pounding rice to make *mochi*, spherical rice cakes.

85

***Kagamibuta* netsuke with rabbits running on waves,**
late 18th century
Wood; 5 cm
Signed: *Yoshikatsu* (school unknown)

According to Chinese mythology, a divine hare-in-the-moon creates the elixir of immortality. And when the full moon causes the oceans to crest, female rabbits conceive by leaping over the waves. Thus, for the Japanese, playful rabbits running over waves became a popular symbol of fertility. This *kagamibuta* netsuke portrays two such rabbits on a pebbly shore with stylized waves breaking behind them.

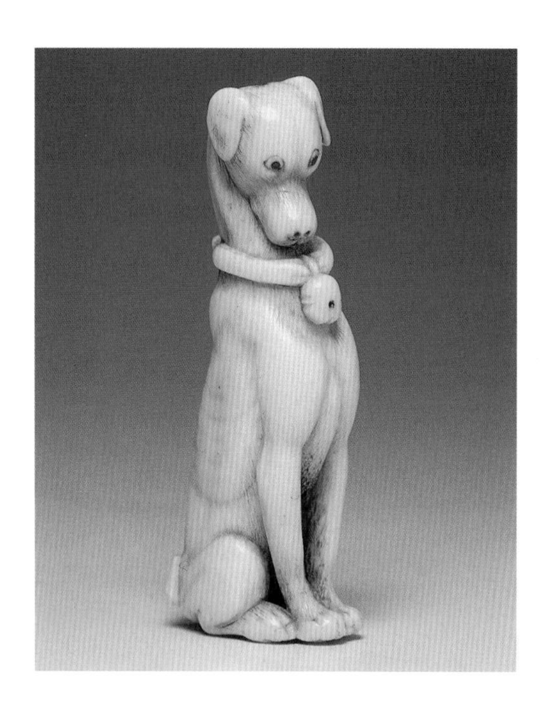

86

Dog, late 18th century
Stag antler; 6 cm
Attributed to Okatomo (Kyoto school)

By cleverly using a narrow section of antler, the artist of this netsuke skillfully portrayed a dog sitting pertly upright with his snout tucked tightly into his chest. To prevent the posture from appearing unnatural, the carver also included a collar and bell to account for the dog's focused attention and stiff carriage. Okatomo might have "borrowed" this design from his master Tomotada, who was known for his depictions of dogs with bell collars. Both artists were extremely accomplished at rendering fur, which is largely worn away in this example.

87

Wild dog with skull, late 18th century
Wood with brass and horn inlays; 3 cm
Signed: *Minkō* (Tanaka Minkō, 1735–1816, Tsu school)

The Japanese venerate wolves and dogs as divine creatures that protect their crops. This emaciated dog, however, recalls Buddhist paintings of dogs in graveyards, picking apart corpses. Such images remind people of life's impermanence and the inevitable decay that awaits all living things. Minkō created many crisply carved, compact designs of animals, which are often benignly humorous. Despite this dog's somewhat protruding ribs, it seems robust with a thick neck and legs and bushy tail. Its expression, too, appears more playful than threatening, more like that of a pet playing with a ball rather than a skull. The red-stained mouth, brass eyes, prominent genitalia, and carefully carved fur characterize much of Minkō's work.

88

Monkey with turtle, late 18th century
Ivory with inlay; 4.3 cm
Signed: *Okatomo* (Kyoto school)

This work shows a clever monkey besting a turtle by grasping its head before it can withdraw into its shell. The netsuke might allude to a story in the *Konjaku monogatari* (Tales of Long Ago), which tells of a tortoise sent to get a monkey's liver to cure an ailing princess. By not revealing his true purpose, the tortoise persuaded the monkey to cross the ocean on his back. When the monkey discovers the plot, he convinces everybody his liver is back on land on a tree branch. When the gullible tortoise returns to get it, the monkey runs away. Zen priests use this parable to illustrate how the Buddha nature is in all of us, just like the monkey's liver was in him all along (Addiss, *The Art of Zen*, pp. 107–8). This netsuke, then, might have been commissioned by a Zen Buddhist or to ward off illness. It might also have commemorated the Asian year of the monkey.

89

Monkey riding catfish, late 18th century
Boxwood; 4 cm
Style of Mitsuhide (Kyoto school)

Zen masters ask their pupils paradoxical questions that will help them get beyond the limitations of reason and depend more on intuition. One of these famous questions, or koans, involves catching "a slippery catfish with a smooth gourd," a seemingly impossible task. Pressing the fish into mud with the gourd will not work, nor will patiently coaxing it into the tiny opening at the gourd's end. This netsuke shows a foolish monkey trying to catch a fish by jumping on its back, a wry comment on the futile efforts of misguided monks. Starting in the early 18th century, folk painters pictured monkeys trying to catch fish as talismans to prevent drowning. This netsuke might have been commissioned for the same reason.

90

Wild dog, late 18th century
Wood with brass inlay; 4.5 cm
Signed: *Kōkei* (Tsu school)

Starting in the late 18th century, netsuke artists frequently depicted dogs, often showing them as *yamainu* (feral dogs or wolves), playful puppies, or exotic breeds. While wild dogs might seem like an unsavory subject, the Japanese associate them with *yama-no-kami*, a mountain god farmers invite into their fields to protect their crops. Such dogs, in fact, although somewhat vicious in appearance, were considered lucky and worthy of respect. For this netsuke, Kōkei closely followed his master Minkō's style of carving *yamainu* with inlaid brass eyes and strong, muscular bodies and legs. Unlike Minkō, however, who usually endowed his male dogs with prominent genitalia, Kōkei pictured this one with his tail tucked between his hind legs, a design that was also popular with such Kyoto artists as Tomotada and Okatomo.

91

Wild dog, late 18th century
Wood with inlay; 5.5 cm
Unsigned

Although boldly carved images of feral dogs, or wolves, known as *yamainu* (literally, "mountain dogs") were commonly executed by Kyoto school artists, especially Tomotada, this netsuke has several distinguishing characteristics. Most notable is the lankiness of the dog's legs, evident even in its seated position. And while Kyoto artists, as well as Tsu school artists like Minkō and Kōkei, finished their dog netsuke by incising them with thousands of tiny lines to suggest fur, this example has been polished smooth. As a result, light plays across the glossy surface, highlighting the beast's protruding ribs and hunched, muscular shoulders. In addition, its unnaturally large eyes and scowling mouth suggest the unworldly nature of *yamainu* as embodiments of the mountain god *yama-no-kami*.

92

Wildcat, late 18th century
Wood with horn inlay; 6 cm
Signed: *Kōkei* (Tsu school)

Wildcats are not common in Japan and can only be found on the small islands of Tsushima, near Nagoya, and Iriomotejima, Okinawa prefecture. Consequently, the artist of this netsuke probably had never seen a wildcat, although he must have been aware of their existence. The creature's untamed nature has been deftly suggested by its crouching posture, intently staring eyes, and long, twitching tail. While Kōkei closely emulated the works of Minkō, his master, he did occasionally develop a new and unusual subject, like this one.

93

Stag, late 18th century
Ivory with horn inlay; 6 cm
Signed: *Yoshitomo* (Kyoto school)

The Chinese believe that deer live for hundreds of years and thus use them as symbols of longevity. In traditional pharmacology, powdered stag horn can be used as a restorative medicine or even an aphrodisiac. The Japanese consider deer to be messengers of the gods and as such keep them within shrine precincts. The deer's mournful cry, suggested here by the animal's open mouth, is also associated with the melancholy of autumn. The carver of this netsuke carefully considered the functional aspect of the object. He tucked the stag's hooves beneath its body and its horns against its back. In that way, no projecting detail can snag the sash or kimono.

94

Toad, late 18th century
Wood with inlay; 5 cm
Attributed to Yasusada Shūzan (Echigo school)

A toad's naturally rounded form makes an ideal netsuke shape since it has no projections that might break off or snag a delicate kimono. To create the bumpy quality of a toad's skin, different netsuke schools developed their own methods. Sukenaga and Sukeyuki (see cat. no. 234) of the Hida school, for example, pitted the wood's surface with regular and minute punctures. The Iwami school artist Tomiharu, as well as Sukesada of the Tsu school, used the laborious *ukibori* technique (see cat. no. 233), whereas the Echigo school artist Shūzan irregularly carved and gouged the material's surface, then polished the raised areas to suggest rounded warts.

The "golden age" of netsuke production occurred during the first half of the 19th century. With Matsudaira Sadanobu's abrupt resignation in 1793 and the death of his faithful successor Matsudaira Nobuakira in 1812, government control fell into the hands of Mizuno Tadanari, a corrupt official who ruled in the name of the shogun Ienari. While the government officially disapproved of the profligate habits of the *chōnin,* it did little to enforce its sumptuary edicts. Ienari himself led the most libidinously extravagant lifestyle of any Tokugawa shogun, indulging in the company of some twenty concubines in addition to his principal wife. As a result, the Bunka (1804–18) and Bunsei (1818–31) eras are often characterized as periods of extreme decadence and ostentatious spending.

This freewheeling consumerism, similar to that of the earlier Genroku (1688–1704) and Temmei (1781–89) eras, greatly boosted netsuke production. Netsuke ateliers that had been established in the 18th century flourished in the hands of second and third generation carvers, who faithfully reproduced the most successful designs of their predecessors and added new subjects and compositions of their own.

Even in the heyday of popular culture in Japan, netsuke artists and their customers continued to enjoy conservative Chinese subject matter. The sanctity of family relationships, especially, remained paramount for the Japanese, and some even wore netsuke representing the Chinese paragons of filial piety (cat. nos. 98 and 99).

A popular movement known as *Shingaku* ("studies of the heart") might have reinforced this interest in Confucian themes. Formulated by Ishida Baigan (1685–1744) and propagated by his followers Tejima Toan (1718–86) and Nakazawa Dōni (1725–1803), Shingaku equated spiritual awakening with an understanding and acceptance of morality. Baigan held that by pursuing money, merchants were merely fulfilling their destiny—a destiny no less honorable than that of the noble samurai, provided they were fair in business and used their profits responsibly and charitably. According to Baigan, merchants ought to be content with their position in society and live frugally and honestly. In so doing, they would help preserve universal harmony (Bellah, *Tokugawa Religion,* pp. 133–77). Thus, netsuke with certain Confucian themes (cat. no. 100) might have reflected these attitudes and their owners' disdain for corruption and profligacy.

At the same time, netsuke artists continued to represent distinctly Japanese subjects. Perhaps out of deference to government bans on depicting current or recent historical events (after the 16th century), netsuke artists tended to portray Japanese heroes of the distant past (cat. nos. 107–9). Curiously enough, the courtesans of the licensed pleasure quarters and the actors of the Kabuki stage—personages that dominated woodblock prints and mirrored the rebellious nature of *chōnin* culture—never became a major theme for netsuke artists. The Japanese figures that do occur often reflect generic types, like sumō wrestlers (cat. no. 119) or courtly dancers (cat. no. 113), and the continuing trend toward greater naturalism.

By the early 19th century, figural designs, however, began to be rivaled by nature themes. Certain schools, in fact, became famous for their nature subjects. Artists working in Gifu and Nagoya, like Tomokazu, excelled at rendering the fine texture of animal hair (cat. nos. 128 and 130). Sukenaga and others of the Hida school in Takayama gained fame for their extremely lifelike frogs and snakes, which were carved from boxwood and carefully stained for a heightened realism. They even rendered a snake's scales individually, rather than in a simple and less effective crosshatch pattern, and experimented with the specialized technique of *ukibori* to accurately depict an amphibian's bumpy texture.

Hidari Issan and Sari (cat. no. 144) of the Iwashiro school specialized in aquatic themes, especially turtles and clusters of shells. Toyomasa and his followers in the Tamba school produced a number of highly original animal designs (cat. nos. 131, 133, and 140), in addition to strange and compelling representations of Taoist immortals (cat. no. 96). In fact, Toyomasa's animals and figures often have large, orblike eyes that are eerily realistic. And while a great variety of netsuke were produced in Kyoto and Osaka, artists in these large cities became known for their nature subjects as well (cat. nos. 135, 138, and 139).

Technical advancements, too, tended to be linked with this early 19th-century quest for greater realism. Many artists, particularly those who specialized in animals, cleverly designed their netsuke with natural openings for the cord, thus eliminating the need for drilling *himotoshi*. Others used a variety of inlays to give their creatures believably glassy and transparent eyes.

The early 19th century, then, can be viewed as the period when Japanese netsuke carving came into its own. Well-patronized ateliers produced a dizzying array of subjects to satisfy the wide-ranging interests and tastes of their customers. At the same time, netsuke artists confidently made their three-dimensional forms all the more lifelike with refined carving techniques and a sophisticated use of materials. Consequently, the craftsmanship and artistic breadth of early 19th-century netsuke proved unparalleled, equaling in their own way the florescence of woodblock printmaking that had taken place a decade or two earlier.

The craftsmanship and artistic breadth of early 19th-century netsuke proved unparalleled, equaling in their own way the florescence of woodblock printmaking that had taken place a decade or two earlier.

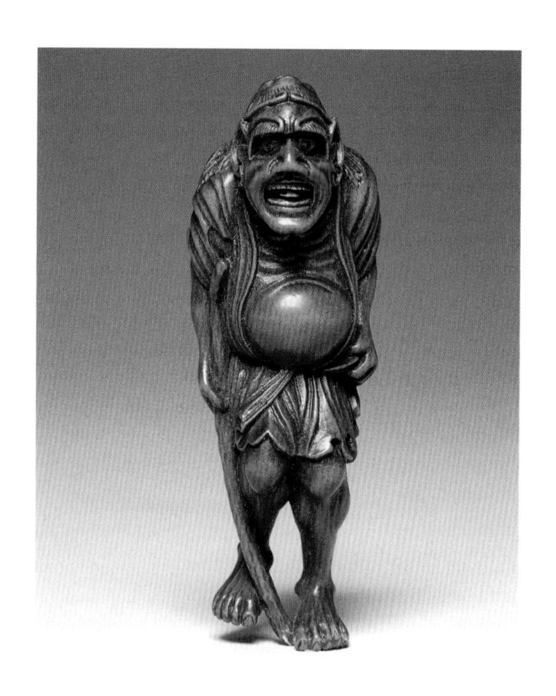

95

Tekkai, early 19th century
Boxwood with ivory inlay; 6 cm
Signed: *Sōshin* (school unknown)

The Chinese Taoist immortal Tekkai (T'ieh-kuai) could exhale his soul from his body and thus travel great distances despite his lameness (see cat. nos. 12 and 13). This figure's smaller scale, greater naturalism, and more anatomically correct proportions all indicate its early 19th-century date. In this rare work, Sōshin heightened the realism by including minute ivory teeth and a tongue. At the same time, he imbued his Tekkai with an other-worldliness by enlivening his robes and giving him grotesque physical features: deeply sunken eyes, a curious ridge across his brow, and strange boil-like bumps on the top of his head.

96

Gama and his toad, early 19th century
Wood with tortoiseshell and horn inlay; 5.3 cm
Signed: *Toyomasa* (1773–1856, Tamba school)

One of the Taoist immortals, Gama (Hsia-mo) had considerable skill in the art of herbal medicine. According to legend, he once caught a white toad while drawing water from a well, and the two became inseparable companions. In this netsuke, Gama laughs openly while the toad crawls over his shoulders and onto his head. Like other Taoist immortals, he has rough features, unkempt hair, and ragged clothing. But unlike earlier renditions that stress the immortals' fantastic nature, this carving possesses a heightened realism achieved through a masterful accumulation of details. Here, for example, Gama's skirt convincingly twists around his waist, and the musculature of his legs, arms, and feet has been painstakingly rendered. Even the teeth in his mouth and the joints of his fingers and toes have been individually carved. The pale tortoiseshell eyes further enliven the figure, giving it an eerie presence.

97

***Niō* guardian with Buddha's sandal**, early 19th century
Wood; 11.2 cm
Signed: *Hosensai* (school unknown)

In India and Southeast Asia, gigantic footprints carved into stone symbolize Buddha Shakyamuni's omniscience and power. The Japanese hang large straw sandals at temple gateways for the same reason. Here, the artist Hosensai cleverly portrayed a *Niō* guardian, which also stands watch at temple entrances, carrying one of Shakyamuni's sandals. Like other early 19th-century netsuke, this miniature tends toward the naturalistic. The *Niō*, for example, differs from earlier examples with their bulging muscles and popping veins (see cat. no. 48) by having a more human physique. The garments, too, hang downward rather than supernaturally blowing about. And instead of having a wrathful expression, which typified earlier representations and was intended to disperse evil, this figure seems comically resigned to his mundane task.

98

Yoko saving his father, early 19th century
Walrus ivory; 4 cm
Signed: *Ikko* (Hasegawa Ikko, Tsu school)

In China, the "twenty-four paragons of filial piety" are people who, through selfless devotion to their parents, epitomize Confucian virtue. Stories about the paragons became extremely important in both China and Japan for fostering a sense of morality among the populace. This netsuke depicts Yoko (Yang Hsiang), who threw himself at an attacking tiger so his father could escape harm. Despite the seriousness of the theme, this miniature seems more whimsical than tragic. Yoko, portrayed as a toddler, appears to be hugging a catlike lion. Meanwhile, his father, pinned beneath the animal, acts more amused than frightened. Multiple figure netsuke like this became especially popular during the 19th century. Its maker, Ikko, was a highly skilled and prolific artist. Working in both ivory and wood, he was particularly adept at carving complex compositions that encourage close examination from all angles. This example is also remarkable for the way one plane seamlessly flows into another.

99

Enshi wearing a deerskin, early 19th century
Wood and lacquered ivory with mother-of-pearl signature plate; 5.4 cm
Signed: *Ryūkei* (Tokyo school)

One of the Chinese "twenty-four paragons of filial piety," Enshi (Yen Tzu) is said to have dressed in a deerskin so he could move undetected in deer herds, milking does for his sick parents. Because of his selfless devotion, he risked being shot by hunters, who would have been unaware of his disguise. In this netsuke, he carries a covered milk bucket while peeking out from the deerskin. The artist Ryūkei excelled at carving figures in a refined and subtle style, but his oeuvre is somewhat obscured by followers who also signed their works with the same art name. Here, for example, Enshi's robes fall in graceful folds while the deerskin, with legs still attached, hangs convincingly across his back and down his sides. Ryūkei increased the netsuke's elegance by fashioning the pail from ivory and painting it with a semitransparent green lacquer.

100

Kyoyū and Sōfu, early 19th century
Ivory; 5 cm
Unsigned

This netsuke depicts a famous episode from the life of Kyoyū (Hsiu Yu), who was renowned for his noble character. According to legend, the emperor Yao once suggested to his councilor Kyoyū that he succeed him to the throne. Kyoyū responded by rushing to a waterfall to wash the potentially corrupting offer out of his ears. When Sōfu (Ch'ao Fu), another lofty sage, heard of Kyoyū's dilemma, he carefully guided his ox upstream so it would not drink the tainted water. This netsuke of the story reflects the early 19th-century trend toward greater compositional complexity. Rather than carving a single figure, the artist created an entire vignette, with such landscape elements as the rocky outcropping where Kyoyū sits to clean his ears, a waterfall, pine trees, and Sōfu's ox. While lacking some of the dramatic impact of earlier works, the miniature provides the viewer with more narrative detail by showing the exact moment when Kyoyū washes his ears and Sōfu pulls his ox away.

101

Hotei and Fukurokuju, early 19th century
Wood; 7 cm
Signed: *Toyomasa* (1773–1856, Tamba school)

This netsuke shows Fukurokuju, the god of longevity, hoisting Hotei (Pu-tai), another god of good fortune, into the air. Fukurokuju is recognizable by his elongated cranium and Hotei by his large stomach and cloth bag. During the Edo period, urban sophisticates recognized the naïveté of worshiping such folk gods and frequently made them the brunt of irreverent humor. Woodblock print artists, for example, utilized the phallic nature of Fukurokuju's extended head and suggestively pictured him with women from the pleasure quarters. In this netsuke, the artist achieved comic effect by transforming Hotei and Fukurokuju into sumō wrestlers wearing only loincloths.

102

Fukurokuju with Chinese child, early 19th century
Wood, ivory, and horn; 6 cm
Signed: *Masakazu* (Yamada-Ise school)

Fukurokuju is often included as one of the Seven Gods of Good Fortune, a group of Chinese deities adopted into Japanese worship in the 15th century. Artists generally portray Fukurokuju with an extremely elongated cranium, probably to suggest his vast wisdom. For this netsuke, Masakazu carved a more traditional image of the god. In his left hand, he holds a staff with a scroll representing his knowledge and in his right hand, a Chinese-style fan. A Chinese child, distinguishable by his costume and top-knots, reaches up adoringly to the old sage. Masakazu's oeuvre is somewhat obscured by the fact that several artists, associated with various schools, all used the same name. The overall sweetness of the figures here, however, together with the distinctive reddish stain, suggests a carver from the Yamada-Ise school.

103

Demon dancing with Okame mask, early 19th century
Wood; 6 cm
Signed: *Deme* (Deme school, Tokyo)

In traditional Chinese and Japanese mythology, horned demons with claws for fingers and toes, known as *oni*, carry out the harsh punishments issued by the King of Hell. Both Chinese and Japanese artists, however, delighted in portraying *oni* as naughty creatures, more comic than monstrous. In this netsuke, a portly *oni* wears a mask representing Okame, the Japanese goddess of fertility, abundance, and mirth. Despite her divinity, Okame is usually shown as homely and somewhat overweight, physical characteristics that humorously match those of this *oni*, with his prodigious stomach and breastlike chest. The maker also emphasized the demon's childlike nature by having him mistakenly tie on the mask upside down. Historically, artists associated with the Deme school produced masks for Nō performances. During the 18th century, however, they began carving finely detailed mask netsuke as well.

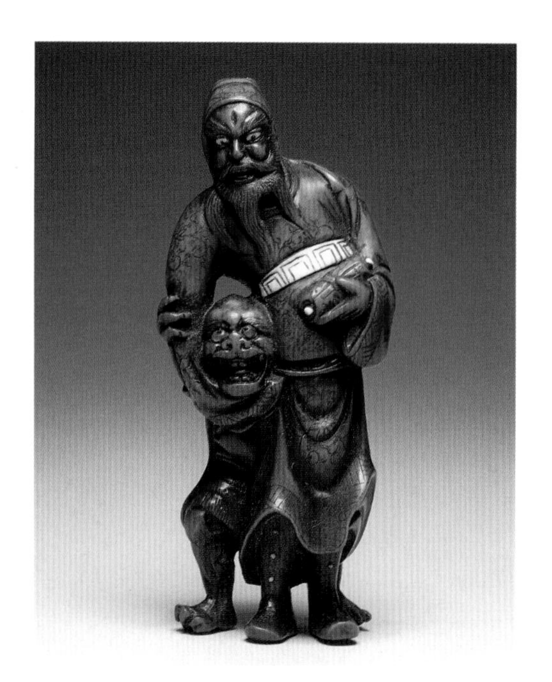

104

Shōki and demon, early 19th century
Wood with ivory, coral, and horn inlays; 8.8 cm
Unsigned

Netsuke artists delighted in showing demons getting the better of Shōki (Chung K'uei), the "demon queller" (see cat. no. 22). This work, however, presents a more sympathetic view of the well-intentioned scholar, showing him as an elegant and commanding person holding an imp in a hammerlock. As was typical of early 19th-century carvings, the figures have naturalistic proportions, musculatures, and poses. Also common to that era is the spare inclusion of different materials for embellishment. Here, for example, ivory has been used for Shōki's eyes and on his boots, belt, and scroll, while a bit of coral (not shown) can be found on his *sagemono*.

105

Demon with Shōki scroll, early 19th century
Ivory; 10 cm
Signed: *Hidemasa* (Osaka school)

As if teaching a class in military preparedness, a horned *oni* points to a hanging scroll with a picture of Shōki (Chung K'uei), the "demon queller." The *oni* may be in for a surprise, however, for this Shōki seems to actually be emerging from the scroll's two-dimensional surface. Even the tassels of his scholar's cap extend beyond the image into the silk mounting. This comical device was not new: woodblock print artists during the 18th century also showed paintings coming to life.

106

Demon, early 19th century
Wood with inlay; 10 cm
Unsigned

According to Buddhist thought, horrible demons known as *oni* carry out the King of Hell's harsh judgments against sinners. During the Edo period (1600–1868), Japanese artists usually depicted *oni* as muscular, compact imps with horns and claws. During the preceding Kamakura (1185–1333) and Muromachi (1392–1573) eras, however, artists showed a much wider range of demonic creatures. In all likelihood, these earlier paintings influenced this netsuke, which features a large-headed demon holding a rosary and carrying a wooden gong.

107

Slaying the *nue*, early 19th century
Ivory; 4.5 cm
Unsigned

The famous 12th-century warrior Minamoto Yorimasa is said to have shot a *nue*, a beast with the head of a monkey, the claws of a tiger, and the tail of a snake, with an arrow. This netsuke shows Yorimasa's retainer, Ii-no-Hayata, finishing the wounded creature off with his sword. As the Japanese government increasingly punished woodblock print artists who designed "morally corrupting" images, "safe" subjects, like the exploits of legendary heroes, became more popular. That trend probably influenced netsuke production, for starting in the early 19th century, netsuke artists, too, portrayed a number of such themes.

108

Nitta-no-Shiro and the boar, early 19th century
Ivory; 5 cm
Unsigned

The lord of Izu province, Nitta-no-Shiro (died 1203), also known as Tadatsune, was a faithful retainer to the shogun Minamoto Yoritomo. According to legend, Nitta-no-Shiro once saved the shogun's life by leaping onto a boar charging toward him. Here, Nitta-no-Shiro sits on the wild beast. Steadying himself by gripping the animal's tail, he thrusts his dagger into its flank.

109

Benkei in a conch shell, early 19th century
Walrus ivory; 6 cm
Unsigned

A militant monk who lived during the 12th century, Benkei became a faithful retainer to the aristocratic warrior Minamoto Yoshitsune during the epic struggle between the Taira and Minamoto families. Artists often depict Benkei in battle or doing something that reveals his legendary strength. This netsuke, however, emphasizes Benkei's role as a *yamabushi*, a priest who venerates mountains as a form of Buddhist worship. He blows on a conch shell, long used by priests to summon worshipers, while emerging from a giant conch.

110

Shiba Onkō, early 19th century
Ivory; 5.5 cm
Signed: *Sōkei* (Ryukyu Islands)

The celebrated Chinese scholar and government official Shiba Onkō (Sze-ma Kuang) is also remembered for an incident that happened during his childhood. When his friend fell into a large water jar, the quick-thinking Shiba did not waste time getting help, but grabbed an ax and broke the jar instead. In this compact 19th-century design, the two boys, rendered in relief, clasp hands and smile happily while water rushes around the child being rescued. Later, somewhat more fussy examples often portray several children crowding around the jar. The increasingly widespread production of netsuke is aptly illustrated by this work's maker, Sōkei. The third generation of a family of carvers, Sōkei is known to have lived in the Ryukyu Islands, south of Kyūshū. He produced full-scale sculptures as well as netsuke (Ducros, "Sokei," pp. 21–25).

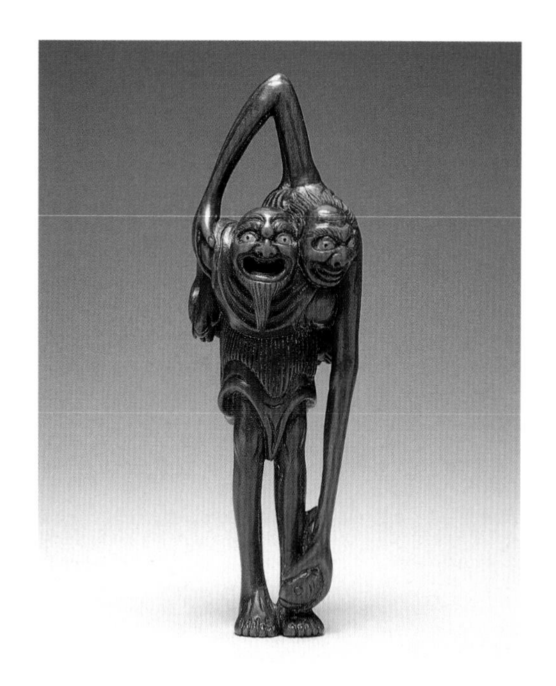

111

Ashinaga and Tenaga, early 19th century
Wood with inlay; 11.5 cm
Unsigned

Along China's Eastern Sea lives a legendary race of people. Those with long legs (Ashinaga) carry their long-armed brothers (Tenaga) on their shoulders into the ocean, where they can snatch fish and other delicacies from the deep water. This theme, which exemplified the benefits of peaceful coexistence, was popular with netsuke artists from early on (see cat. no. 60), perhaps because the figures' long limbs naturally created the attenuated compositions so favored during the 18th century. Several aspects of this netsuke, however, as well as catalogue number 112, reveal its early 19th-century date. In both works, the arms and legs have been mostly carved away from the base material, resulting in large areas of "negative" space. The faces, too, have more humorous expressions than earlier representations, an effect made more pronounced here by the figures' inlaid eyes.

112

Ashinaga and Tenaga, early 19th century
Ivory; 12.4 cm
Unsigned

In a clever variation on the Ashinaga and Tenaga theme, the figures in this work have been shown in a comical predicament. An octopus has tightly wrapped its tentacles around Ashinaga's ankle. When Tenaga reaches down to remove it, he also becomes ensnared. Thus, the two struggle to maintain their balance, while the frowning octopus determinedly maintains its grip.

113

Butterfly dancer, early 19th century
Wood; 7.3 cm
Unsigned

One of the earliest theatrical dances in Japan, Bugaku included several pieces performed by children, including *kochō*, the butterfly dance. In the classic 11th-century novel *Genji monogatari* (Tales of Genji), page girls and boys dressed in fanciful costumes with colorful wings perform the dance of butterflies and sparrows. This netsuke portrays a butterfly dancer, wearing a loose, long-sleeved garment and wings on his back. The netsuke's cord would have passed through a *himotoshi* in the figure's stomach and under his right arm. Thus when worn, the dancer would have faced the owner's body, and only the butterfly wings and leaf-shaped train would have been visible (see back cover).

114

Hunter with squirrel, early 19th century
Wood, ivory, horn, and malachite; 12.5 cm
Unsigned

The meaning of this netsuke remains unclear. Like 18th-century portrayals of famous Taoist immortals, this tall figure has a craggy face and wears a skirt made from leaves. But instead of leaning on a staff, he carries a long-barreled rifle. Most mysterious of all, he holds a live squirrel, presumably his quarry. The hunter has been further "updated" by the inclusion of two *sagemono* that were fashionable during the Edo period: a gourd container with a Daruma netsuke and a tobacco pouch with a *manjū* netsuke.

115

Dutchman with child, early 19th century
Wood; 8.5 cm
Unsigned

Under its strict policy of isolationism, the Tokugawa government forbade the Japanese to travel abroad and foreigners to visit Japan. It did, however, grant the Dutch trading privileges, but restricted them to the small island of Deshima, off the coast of Nagasaki. Except for government officials, no one was allowed to have contact with the Europeans. Consequently, their exotic clothing and odd customs, viewed only from afar, became intriguing to the curious. Like other Japanese artists, netsuke makers often had to base their depictions of the foreigners on woodblock prints from Nagasaki, which were sold as souvenirs. Unlike early 18th-century carvers, who produced tall, unnaturally rigid figures, 19th-century artists achieved a much greater realism by showing their subjects in a variety of poses. Here, a smiling father bends downward to allow his small son to climb onto his shoulders.

116

Dutchman putting on a shoe, early 19th century
Ivory with inlay; 4.5 cm
Unsigned

Like catalogue number 115, this netsuke possesses a convincing degree of naturalism by showing a Dutchman bending at the waist and hunching his shoulders forward to awkwardly put on his shoes from a standing position. But rather than the typical caricatured face, the countenance here more closely resembles portraiture. Characteristically, however, the artist carefully noted details of the foreigner's costume, including the rough texture of his woolen socks and the buttons on the side and back of his tunic.

117

Dutchman and goat, early 19th century
Ivory, jadeite, metal, horn, and amber; 13.5 cm
Unsigned

With its "blank" stare, stylized ringlets of hair, and impossibly tall proportions, this netsuke closely mimics the elongated figures popular during the 18th century. The artist's striking use of color and precious inlays, however, foreshadows the sophisticated designs that would become fashionable during the 19th century. The inclusion of an anatomically correct goat also suggests a 19th-century date, although the reason for pairing a Dutchman with a goat remains unknowable. Possibly, the artist specialized in carving foreigners and wanted to create a netsuke that would commemorate the year of the goat as well.

118

Warrior and helmet, early 19th century
Wood with horn and stag antler inlays; 6 cm
Unsigned

High-ranking feudal lords began to wear extremely ornate helmets during Japan's Momoyama period (1568–1600). Here, a scowling warrior sports a complex helmet with fantastic creatures on the bowl, and bamboo and plum patterns on the neck guards. This netsuke once belonged to the famous London collector W. L. Behrens. Sometime after 1913, the warrior's head and helmet were sold separately. The current owner discovered the head in Toledo in 1974. Six years later, he bought the helmet in Los Angeles.

119
Sumō wrestlers, early 19th century
Wood; 7.5 cm
Unsigned

Following the vogue for woodblock prints of sumō wrestlers, netsuke artists first began to produce carvings of the subject during the second half of the 18th century. At the time, Japanese art had begun to reflect Western ideas of scientific and anatomical accuracy, and the wrestlers' near-naked bodies provided artists with a good opportunity to explore these concepts. While the bulkiness of these figures resembles earlier netsuke, other elements, like the careful attention to the wrestlers' musculature and straining tendons, suggest an early 19th-century date. Despite the top heaviness of the piece, caused by one fighter lifting the other off the ground, the artist achieved a remarkable balance, letting the figures stand solidly on their own as would become popular later in the century with *okimono,* larger, freestanding sculptures.

120
Shishi, early 19th century
Boxwood with ivory inlay; 4 cm
Signed: *Masasada* (Tamba school)

Although 19th-century netsuke carvers began to depict native Japanese subjects, they also continued to make miniatures of Chinese immortals and mythical animals. The Tamba school artist Masasada fashioned this *shishi*—with its curling mane and tail—in an active, albeit conventional, pose. He achieved a degree of novelty, however, by giving the beast a catlike quality, comically portraying it standing on the balls of its paws. He inlaid each retracted claw with a bit of ivory and further demonstrated his skill by carving a round, free-moving jewel in the "cage" of the *shishi*'s mouth.

121

Fox priest, early 19th century

Lacquered wood; 8.5 cm

Signed: *Shūzan* (Nagamachi Shūzan, Osaka school)

The Japanese think foxes possess supernatural powers, including the ability to change themselves into human form. In the popular Kyōgen play *Tsurigitsune*, an old fox changes into a priest to escape being hunted (see cat. no. 69). The carver of this priest fox was Nagamachi Shūzan, a follower of the famous Yoshimura Shūzan. Although there are few similarities in the style and subjects of their works, both painted the surfaces of their wood netsuke. But while Yoshimura Shūzan gained renown for his superb composite beasts, Nagamachi Shūzan produced a number of roughly carved figures in the rustic *ittobori* technique. This example, however, has sophisticated carving and expert painting. Shūzan embellished the priest's somber robes with a delicate cloud pattern in red lacquer.

122

***Tanuki* metamorphosis**, early 19th century

Wood; 7 cm

Unsigned

The Japanese believe that *tanuki*, raccoonlike dogs, possess supernatural powers, including the ability to change their shape. It is said that *tanuki* liked to wrap themselves in lotus leaves and transform into poor priests, thus tricking people into giving them food and money. This ambitious netsuke portrays such a metamorphosis, with the *tanuki*'s paws changing into hands and feet, and its leaf robe and cap into vestments.

123

***Tengu* hatchling**, early 19th century
Wood; 5 cm
Unsigned (Tamba school)

The origins of the Japanese *tengu*, a birdlike creature with human characteristics, remains unclear. Some scholars hypothesize that they derive from the Chinese *t'ien-kou*, a vicious "celestial dog" that lives deep in the mountains. Others associate them with the Indian *garuda*, which were guardians of the Buddhist faith and had the heads and wings of birds and the bodies of men. Regardless, the Japanese believe *tengu* possess enormous martial abilities. In fact, the great 12th-century warrior Yoshitsune is said to have learned the art of war from Sōjōbō, the *tengu*'s powerful leader. This netsuke shows a *tengu* hatchling struggling to free itself from its egg. Its fierce expression and muscled arms indicate its bellicose nature.

124

***Tengu* on a feather fan**, early 19th century
Ivory and coral; 4.8 cm
Unsigned (Osaka school)

Perhaps because *tengu* were birdlike creatures who lived deep in the mountains, they became emblematic of *yamabushi*, wandering priests who venerate mountains. The one here wears the wide leggings and vest of a *yamabushi*. He crouches on a fan made from seven crow feathers, a prestige object associated with Sōjōbō, the mythical leader of the *tengu*.

125

***Tengu* with a broken wing**, early 19th century
Ivory with horn inlay; 4 cm
Unsigned (Osaka school)

This humorous netsuke portrays an unlucky *tengu* with a broken wing. Covering his face in despair, he holds the detached appendage in his right hand. He wears an *eboshi*, a small lacquered cap used by *yamabushi*, itinerant Buddhist priests. As is typical of works by the Osaka school, this carving displays a gentle humor and sympathetic portrayal of animals. The rounded feathers and sad, drooping eyes with inlaid pupils follow the style of Garaku, an artist who was mentioned in Inaba Tsūryū's *Sōken Kishō* as being active during the third quarter of the 18th century. Perhaps the maker of this piece was familiar with Garaku's netsuke.

126

Palace of the clam's dream, early 19th century
Ivory; 4 cm
Signed: *Kagetoshi* (Kyoto school)

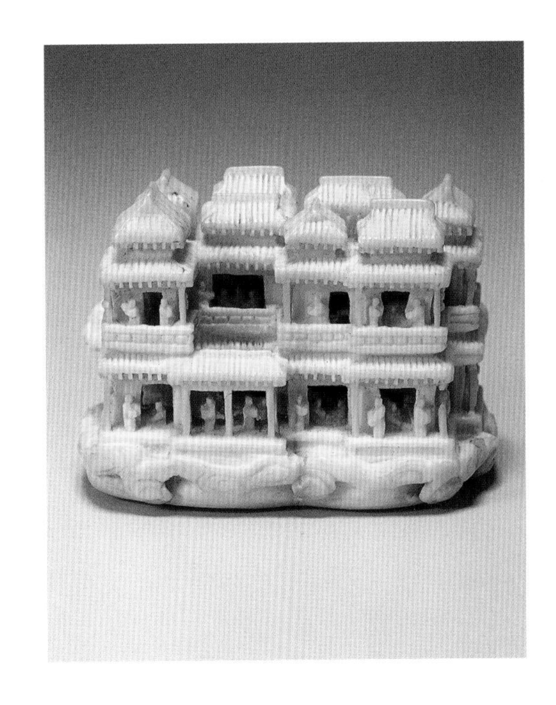

According to Chinese folk beliefs, the Dragon King rules the seas from a magnificent palace deep beneath the waves. Part of his power derived from a pair of magic jewels, which he used to control the ebb and flow of the tides. It is even said that when a clam opened, it emitted a mist containing a vision of his abode. Netsuke carvers were fond of showing the Dragon King's palace inside the separated halves of a clam shell, as if it were within the clam's "dream." The versatile and often highly original Kyoto artist Kagetoshi produced a number of such compositions using the difficult openwork technique of *sukashibori*. In this one, he not only carved the palace in astounding detail, but included numerous tiny figures in the rooms.

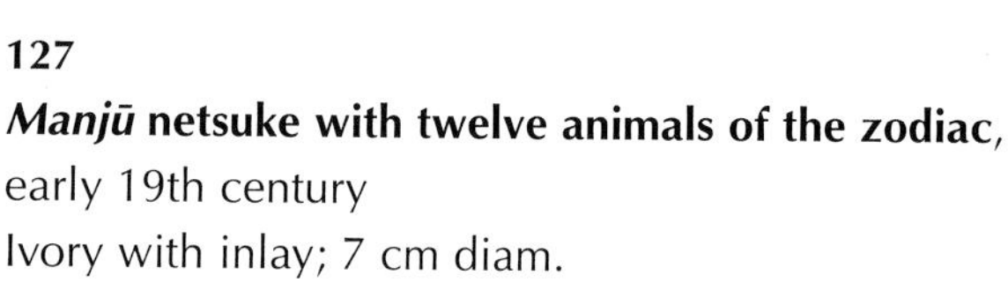

127

***Manjū* netsuke with twelve animals of the zodiac,**
early 19th century
Ivory with inlay; 7 cm diam.
Signed: *Ikko* (Hasegawa Ikko, Tsu school)

All twelve animals of the Asian zodiac adorn the surface of this *manjū*-shaped netsuke. Despite the complex composition, Ikko masterfully delineated each beast by deeply carving the surrounding material. And although the creatures surrealistically intertwine, he carefully avoided any unnatural distortion by rendering each one in a believable pose. In addition, he lightly stained the surface and inlaid the eyes of the tiger and the dragon with whiter pieces to distinguish them as the two most powerful. He also used bits of black horn for the pupils, thereby creating effective accents in this churning sea of animals and ivory. Perhaps to lighten the piece, he hollowed out the back. It is also possible that the uncarved bowl was used as an ash holder. As such, it would have been part of an ensemble that traditionally included a tobacco pouch (*tonkotsu*) and a pipe holder (*kiseruzutsu*).

128

Rat on chestnut, early 19th century
Wood with inlay; 3.8 cm
Signed: *Tomokazu* (about 1765–1840, Gifu school)

According to Japanese lore, the rat is the first animal of the Asian zodiac and the messenger of Daikoku, a god of grain. As such, artists often show rats reaping autumn's harvest by attacking ripened rice and millet or, as seen here, chestnuts. As a result, their presence symbolized bounty instead of infestation, and netsuke of them were considered acceptable objects of personal adornment. Tomokazu seems to have been especially fond of carving rats, as many by him exist. In fact, his creatures, in both scale and demeanor, are more like adorable mice. Here, he contrasted the finely rendered fur of the animal with the smoothness of the chestnut and its roughly pitted top.

129

Tiger, early 19th century
Wood; 4.5 cm
Unsigned

The third animal of the Asian zodiac, the tiger symbolizes strength and power, and people born under its sign are thought to be passionate, daring, and somewhat unpredictable. Since tigers were not indigenous to Japan, early artists had to imagine how they looked by examining imported hides or European book illustrations. As a result, Japanese depictions of tigers often resemble domesticated house cats. By the 19th century, even though they were undoubtedly aware of the tiger's true nature, Japanese artists continued to produce amusingly benign representations of them in great numbers. The oversized feet and small head of this animal make it slightly comical, but its hunched posture and hungry gaze seem convincingly threatening.

130

Monkey eating persimmons, early 19th century
Wood with inlay; 3.8 cm
Signed: *Tomokazu* (about 1765–1840, Gifu school)

In addition to rats, Tomokazu excelled at depicting monkeys, usually devouring fruit. Here, a lucky monkey holds a persimmon in its hands while clutching a branch with two more in its feet. Like other monkey netsuke by Tomokazu, the animal convincingly bites the fruit with the side of its mouth. The intent eyes are slightly crossed and rendered with double inlays. Tomokazu carved the fur in his typically fine manner and stained it a dark brown. He colored the monkey's face and ears, as well as the persimmons, with a lighter, reddish hue.

131
Monkey, early 19th century
Wood with inlay; 3.5 cm
Signed: *Namboku* (Tamba school)

The ninth animal of the Asian zodiac, the monkey, although mischievous, is considered lucky. This netsuke shows a melodramatically pensive one, with its hands covering its head, eyes downcast, and feet clenched nervously beneath it. The monkey's compact posture creates a perfectly functional netsuke— smooth, round, and easily pushed beneath the sash. This ingenious design was probably first carved by Namboku's master, Toyomasa. Like him, Namboku inlaid the monkey's eyes with light, translucent horn, or tortoiseshell, and dark pupils.

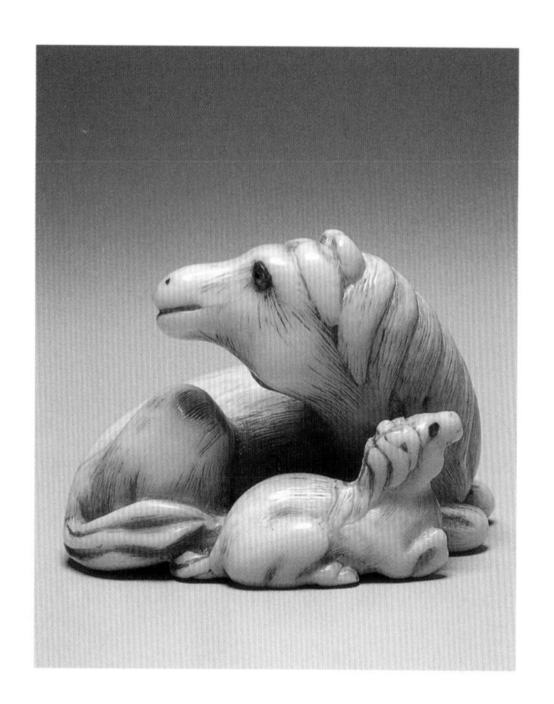

132
Mare and foal, early 19th century
Ivory with inlay; 4 cm
Style of Rantei (Kyoto school)

Horses have long been revered in China and Japan, where they are synonymous with military expansion, conquest, and prestige. Artists in both countries have produced countless depictions of them as noble and spirited beasts. Netsuke carvers, however, preferred to make more bucolic renditions of them, often showing them recumbent with their legs tucked neatly beneath them. This ivory example depicts a mare sheltering her foal.

133

Ox, early 19th century

Wood with inlay; 4.7 cm

Signed: *Toyomasa* (1773–1856, Tamba school)

For centuries, Japanese and Chinese artists have used large, lumbering oxen as emblems of a bucolic existence, far from the din and turmoil of urban life. They also frequently pictured oxen, or waterbuffalo, as the vehicles of revered sages and scholars. For example, Roshi (Lao-tzu), the founder of Taoism, rides upon an ox. In Japanese handscrolls, oxen commonly pull the two-wheeled carriages (*gissha*) of aristocrats. The most compelling story tells of a Heian statesman and poet, whose ox died of grief while bearing his dead master to the funeral pyre. For this netsuke, Toyomasa conventionally posed the animal as recumbent, with its legs tucked underneath and its head turned back, thus creating a compact and rounded form. He masterfully invigorated this ox, however, by having it raise its right foreleg, as if it were about to stand.

134

Goat, early 19th century

Ivory with inlay; 4 cm

Unsigned

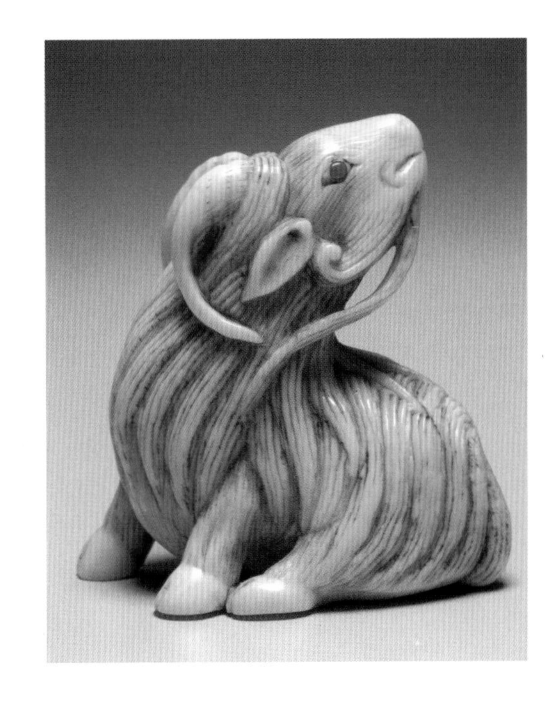

Goats were not native to Japan and rarely occur as artistic themes. Through contact with the Chinese, however, the Japanese must have become aware of them at an early date, especially since the goat, or sheep, is the eighth animal of the Asian zodiac. For that reason, the goat frequently became the subject of netsuke carvers, especially for those who specialized in animal themes, like Tomotada, Tomokazu, Minkō, and Kōkei. This goat has been depicted in a state of movement, rising to examine something that has caught its attention. Its horns have been placed against the back of its neck, eliminating the possibility of their sharp tips snagging the delicate material of the kimono or sash.

135

Dog, early 19th century
Ivory with inlay; 4.2 cm
Signed: *Hakuryū* (Kyoto school)

This dog probably represents one of several, sturdy varieties of short hairs that were domesticated in Japan at an early time. Such dogs were used for hunting and for sport, like dog fights and *inuoumono,* a game in which mounted archers tried to shoot a running dog before it escaped the playing field. While this netsuke was probably worn to commemorate the Asian year of the dog, it might also have reflected the owner's enthusiasm for *kemari,* a game in which players keep a ball aloft with their feet. Here, the dog rests its paw on a *kemari* ball, incised around its circumference with the leather strip used to lash the two halves together.

136

Dog and pup, early 19th century
Wood; 5.3 cm
Signed: *Minkō* (school unknown)

This dog's lankiness and emaciated condition recall late 18th-century depictions of *yamainu,* divine "mountain dogs" (see cat. no. 91). But the artist's attention to anatomy and emphasis on procreation (the curly tailed puppy) make this an accurate nature study and typical of carvings from the 19th century. Stylistically, too, this miniature is very different from 18th-century netsuke. Stocky, broad-pawed dogs became associated with the late 18th-century Tsu artist Minkō (see cat. no. 87). This one was probably done by a 19th-century artist who used the same name.

137

Hen and chicks, early 19th century
Wood with horn inlay; 5 cm
Signed: *Masatomo* (Nagoya school)

The tenth animal of the Asian zodiac, the rooster is usually represented as a proud cockerel with luxurious tail feathers. And while netsuke like this might have been purchased to commemorate the year of the rooster, it seems more likely that buyers simply were fond of such regal birds. Japanese and Chinese artists alike often pictured ornithological subjects, and carefully rendered, realistic paintings of birds became especially popular in 18th-century Japan under the influence of Shen Nan-p'in, a Chinese artist who visited there between 1731 and 1733. By the third quarter of the 18th century, Japanese netsuke makers depicted hens and chickens in addition to roosters. This work, in fact, probably was based on an earlier carving by the Kyoto artist Okatomo, who was famous for his expert renditions of quail and other birds.

138

Falcon and catfish, early 19th century
Ivory with inlay; 4 cm
Signed: *Shūōsai* (Osaka school)

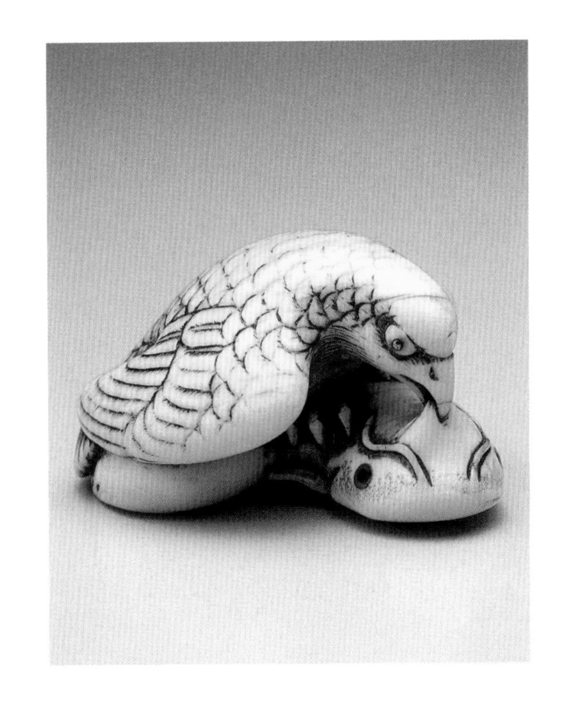

Japanese artists began to paint birds of prey during the Muromachi period (1333–1573), probably inspired by images from China. The subject appealed to aristocrats and warriors, for whom falconry had long been a favorite pastime. During the Edo period, common townspeople also purchased woodblock prints of the proud, fierce birds. This well-worn netsuke shows a falcon beginning to devour a catfish. The artist faithfully reproduced the way such birds lift their wings during combat. He also cleverly inlaid the falcon's eyes with metal, giving them a cold, cruel look.

139

Snake, early 19th century
Ivory with horn inlay; 5 cm
Signed: *Kagetoshi* (Kyoto school)

In Japanese myth and legend, snakes are both the benevolent manifestations of Shinto gods, especially those associated with the ocean and life-giving rains, and large, evil serpents that terrorize people. As the sixth creature of the zodiac, the snake became a popular subject for netsuke artists, who must have been interested in its complicated, knotlike coiling and smooth, scaled skin. Individual artists developed their own methods of rendering scales, with the least skilled simply carving crisscross patterns. The Kyoto master Kagetoshi, who was best known for his astoundingly detailed renderings of miniature palaces (see cat. no. 126), made this remarkably lifelike netsuke. He represented each scale of the snake's body and then arranged its coils in an irregular manner, which invites repeated examination of the object from all sides.

140

Turtle, early 19th century
Wood and horn; 4.7 cm
Signed: *Toyomasa* (1773–1856, Tamba school)

The tortoise has always symbolized longevity in Taoist mythology. But the artist here was more intent on realistically rendering a common box turtle. With extreme precision, Toyomasa depicted the domed panes of the creature's carapace, the scaly texture of its skin, and the peculiar way its head and appendages telescope in and out. To relieve the geometric regularity of the turtle's shell, he carved its head with a subtle turn to the right. Wonderfully objective and well observed, this carving attests to Toyomasa's great skill and stands apart from many of his works, which depict eerie, otherworldly beings.

141

Turtles, early 19th century
Wood; 3.5 cm
Signed: *Tadatoshi* (Nagoya school)

For this amusing netsuke, Tadatoshi carved several turtles, one on top of the other as if vying for the best exposure to the sun. In his meticulous attention to detail, Tadatoshi surpassed his master Tametaka, thus establishing the Nagoya school as a competitive supplier of fine nature studies. In this miniature, Tadatoshi fashioned narrow spaces between the animals' shells, so each is fully in the round and bears its weight realistically on its own legs. The creatures' hard shells, rough skin, and distinctive beaklike heads have all been accurately described. Even the bumpy plastrons, or undersides, of the three largest turtles have been effectively realized with the *ukibori* technique.

142

Toad on a twisted root, early 19th century
Wood with horn inlay; 9 cm
Signature undeciphered

As the cosmic symbol of the moon and a companion to the immortal Gama (Hsia-mo), the toad features prominently in both Japanese and Chinese mythology. This representation, however, is more naturalistic than metaphysical. The artist emphasized the toad's angular bone structure and bumpy skin as natural camouflage, placing it against a piece of knotty driftwood. Years of wear have enhanced the netsuke tactilely and visually—polishing the high points and creating a glistening surface suggestive of a damp bog.

143

***Fugu* (Globefish)**, early 19th century
Wood with ivory and coral; 4 cm
Signed: *Santo* (Santo Toman, probably Tokyo school)

The Japanese have long considered *fugu*, a kind of globefish, to be a culinary delicacy. Beyond its subtle taste, however, the fish also possesses an element of risk. If improperly prepared, it can become contaminated from toxins in its liver, making it fatal if eaten. Netsuke artists also found the dangerous *fugu* intriguing as a subject because of its unusual ability to inflate itself. This charming *fugu*, however, appears both comical and shy. It looks upward while its tail sweeps to one side against its body, helping to produce the netsuke's rounded, functional form. The artist used the *ukibori* technique to accurately reproduce the subtle texture of the creature's underside.

144

Shells, early 19th century
Wood; 3.8 cm
Signed: *Sari* (Iwashiro school)

By wearing a netsuke of a zodiac animal, the owner could commemorate the coming of a new year and display his fastidious attention to the latest fashion. Other less obvious themes also had similar purposes. For example, in 1809, the year of the snake, a private Japanese poetry society commissioned the woodblock print artist Ryūryūkyo Shinsai to design a series of images on shells. The island of Enoshima was not only a popular place for gathering shells but was famous for its shrine to Benten, a goddess of music, literature, and love. Since one of her attributes is a white snake, a somewhat labyrinthine association between snakes and shells came into being. Twelve years later during the next year of the snake, Hokusai was also asked to produce a set of thirty-six shell prints (Keyes, *The Art of Surimono*, pp. 35–37). Thus, this skillfully realized netsuke might also have been commissioned to herald the year of the snake.

145

Gourd, early 19th century

Ivory; 6.7 cm

Unsigned

From early on, both the Chinese and Japanese used large, dried gourds with their hollow interiors to carry water or liquor and smaller ones to hold powdered medicine. Such gourds, in fact, were a common *sagemono*, together with tobacco pouches and coin purses. This ivory netsuke of a gourd has been made more interesting by the skillful reticulation of the material to create the plant's twisting stem and leaves.

146

Box-shaped (*hako*) netsuke with *katabami*,

early 19th century

Lacquer; 4.3 cm diam.

Signed: *Yōyūsai* (Hara Yōyūsai, 1772–1845, Tokyo)

Artists also made netsuke shaped like the small, circular boxes used to store incense. The cord passes through a hole in the bottom of the box and attaches to an eyelet on the underside of the lid. This box netsuke features three crests with pine boughs. The crests, stylized renditions of the wood-sorrel flower (*katabami*), have pointed sword tips between the petals. These crests undoubtedly reflect the military interests of the owner. The netsuke's maker, Yōyūsai, was a highly skilled lacquer artist whose patrons tended to be aristocrats. This example, however, with its conservative, heraldic form of ornamentation, typifies sets of lacquerware commissioned by feudal warlords.

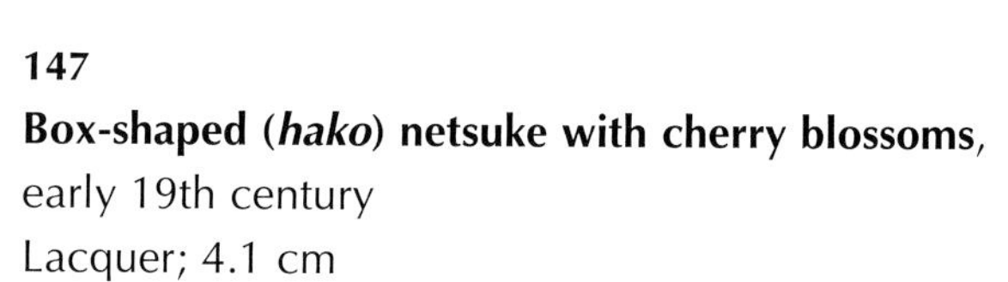

147

Box-shaped (*hako*) netsuke with cherry blossoms,
early 19th century
Lacquer; 4.1 cm
Signed: *Kajikawa* (Tokyo)

When Japanese aristocrats and high-ranking families went on picnics to enjoy the seasons, they strung decorative curtains between trees to create temporary shelters. Such enclosures protected them from annoying breezes and prying eyes. This box netsuke echoes the shape of one of those curtains and features blossoming cherry trees. It has been signed with the name Kajikawa, a family of lacquer artists patronized by the ruling Tokugawa family. Even in this relatively small example, details have been exquisitely wrought. The background, seen on the box's sides, has been rendered in the *nashiji* technique of lightly sprinkled gold, whereas the curtain and cherry tree have been carved in slight relief (*takamake*). The curtain itself, colored with two shades of gold, has been further embellished with a dragon-and-cloud design often found on elaborate Chinese brocades.

148

Mokugyo, early 19th century
Ivory with mother-of-pearl, coral, and horn; 3.5 cm
Signed: *Sankoken* (school unknown)

Comprised of objects associated with Buddhism, this netsuke takes the overall form of a *mokugyo*, a hollow spherical gong. Buddhist monks strike *mokugyo* to keep time for chanting. Such gongs are usually carved from wood to resemble two-headed fish, with the heads meeting to create a handle. Because fish never seem to close their eyes, they symbolize humankind's quest for enlightenment. This netsuke, however, represents a broken *mokugyo*, for the back is missing, revealing the gong's interior with a spider clinging to it. While the artist might have wanted to suggest the transient nature of all things with an appropriate Buddhist symbol, he also might have been alluding to the decline and corruption of the Buddhist church in Japan.

The free-spending decadence and corruption that had marked the early 19th century quickly eroded previous attempts at economic and social reforms. The government covered its debts by debasing currency, but that tactic gave rise to runaway inflation. In turn, feudal lords who needed cash pressured their tenant farmers to produce more rice. But a series of crop failures between 1824 and 1832 brought about widespread famine and led to peasant uprisings in both the countryside and the cities. As a result, Mizuno Tadakuni, senior councilor to the shogun Ieyoshi, initiated a new series of reforms between 1841 and 1843.

Named after the era (1830–44) in which they were enacted, the Tempō Reforms, like the previous Kyōhō and Kansei reforms, attempted to remedy the country's economic ills by endorsing a return to the Confucian values of self-sacrifice and frugality. The government exhorted feudal lords to live more simply and to increase their agricultural yield by cultivating more land. It also forbade peasants, under penalty of death, to migrate to the cities and forced wealthy merchants and moneylenders to give "loans" to the shogunate as an expression of their nationalism.

These attempts to restrict public spending and dictate morality resulted in some of the harshest sumptuary laws ever enforced. In 1842, the government closed all brothels in Edo except those in the Yoshiwara district. Such related businesses as hairdressing and gambling also were forbidden. Stages for public entertainment (*yose*) were reduced from 125 to fifteen (Nishiyama, *Edo Culture*, p. 240), and Kabuki theaters were prohibited from staging elaborately designed plays. Depictions of Kabuki actors and beautiful courtesans—standard subjects for woodblock prints—were banned as well.

How the Tempō Reforms impacted netsuke production is difficult to ascertain. Like previous sumptuary restrictions, the reforms advised *chōnin* against wearing luxurious clothing and hairstyles, but the new laws did not mention netsuke and *sagemono*. And while the reforms were strictly administered, they were not long-lived; Tadakuni was forced to resign in 1844 after his abolition of merchant monopolies and wholesale organizations backfired, leading to food shortages and even higher inflation. Nevertheless, the Tempō Reforms might have inadvertently increased netsuke production as wealthy townsmen searched for discreet ways to spend large sums of money on status objects. The small size and basic functionality of netsuke might have also helped them to be overlooked, even by government spies.

At mid-century, netsuke artists tended to favor a certain preciousness in their designs, fashioning smaller works in greater detail. In Edo, for example, Hōjitsu (cat. nos. 154 and 165) and Jugyoku (cat. no. 201) combined various materials in a single piece, an approach that imbued their carvings with added interest and called attention to their astonishingly high level of workmanship. Other Edo artists increasingly used valuable inlays to embellish their netsuke. Followers of the late 18th-century Tokyo artist Shibayama Senzō, for instance, encrusted the surfaces of their netsuke with rare inlays for both decorative and overtly opulent effects.

Similarly, two artists in Osaka gained fame for their superhuman craftsmanship. Kaigyokusai carved difficult compositions in microscopic detail with the finest materials available (cat. nos. 169, 177, and 192). And Mitsuhiro delighted his patrons with the relatively pristine surfaces of his designs (cat. nos. 153 and 182), which were often so finely stained and polished that the substances they were made from were not easily identifiable.

Like woodblock print artists, netsuke carvers seem to have avoided controversial subject matter. While erotic netsuke were produced (cat. no. 156), netsuke with politically subversive content were rare. Nature and legendary and mythical Chinese and Japanese subjects continued to predominate, but ghosts, supernatural creatures, and other bizarre topics also became motifs for netsuke artists. These trends echoed the popularity of such themes with print artists. In 1830, for example, Katsushika Hokusai published his series of *One Hundred Ghost Tales* (*Hyaku monogatari*). In 1865, Tsukioka Yoshitoshi printed his *One Hundred Supernatural Tales of Japan and China* (*Wakan hyaku monogatari*) and between 1887 and 1892, his *Thirty-six Ghosts and Demons* (*Shinkei sanjurokkaisen*). As a result, netsuke depicting animals with supernatural powers, like *tanuki* (cat. no. 167) and foxes, or entirely imaginary creatures, like *kappa* (cat. no. 168) and *tengu* (cat. no. 162), began to be made in great numbers.

At mid-century, netsuke artists tended to favor a certain preciousness in their designs, fashioning smaller works in greater detail.

149

Handaka and dragon, mid-19th century
Ivory; 4.4 cm
Signed: *Hakusai* (Asakusa school, Tokyo)

Handaka (Panthaka) is one of the sixteen original followers of Shakyamuni, the historic Buddha. An Indian ascetic who lived in the wilderness, Handaka is often pictured with a dragon as his companion. This carving shows the dragon cradling him with his serpentine body, while a mysterious vapor rises from Handaka's begging bowl. The reverse includes the dragon's tail and one of his three-clawed feet grasping a cosmic jewel. Despite the complicated *ryūsa* openwork, Hakusai created a rounded and compact composition that functioned well as a netsuke.

150

***Kagamibuta* netsuke with Kannon on a carp**,
mid-19th century
Ivory with inlay; 4.3 cm
Signed: *Hakusai* (Asakusa school, Tokyo)

Buddhists believe that a *bodhisattva* is an enlightened being who has postponed entering nirvana to help others. The most popular *bodhisattva* is Kannon (Kuan-yin), who is seen here riding on a giant carp. Artists often portray Kannon with female characteristics because of his extreme compassion for others. The center of this netsuke shows the boy Sudhana, who sought Kannon's spiritual guidance. The reverse has been carved to resemble a decaying lotus leaf and flowerless pod. A standard symbol for Buddhist purity, the lotus here also suggests the inevitable decline of all living things and reminds the faithful to attend to their salvation. Hakusai added an element of subtle humor by picturing a frog emerging from a tear in the leaf.

151

Daruma, mid-19th century

Wood with ivory and horn inlays; 3.5 cm

Signed: *Tokuju* (school unknown)

According to Zen beliefs, a Brahman prince known as Daruma (Bodhidharma) traveled from India to China in the early 6th century to spread Buddhist teachings. By emphasizing meditation as a way to achieve enlightenment, Daruma founded the Ch'an, or Zen, sect in Asia. After his death, Daruma became associated with many extraordinary feats, including meditating for nine years while facing a cave wall. During that time, his legs atrophied and withered away. In referring to this story, Japanese children's toys representing Daruma are often shaped like eggs and weighted to right themselves when pushed over. This netsuke echoes the shape of such toys, but Daruma's tormented expression also captures the physical anguish he endured to attain enlightenment. The artist made the figure's startling visage all the more powerful by the high level of detail he included, such as the minute teeth and uvula of the sage's mouth.

152

Hotei and child, mid-19th century

Wood; 3.3 cm

Signed: *Masatoshi* (1835–84, Nagoya school)

Because of his capricious nature, the 9th-century Buddhist monk Hotei (Pu-tai) was associated with children and often shown as their oversized playmate. Here, he happily bends over while a small boy passes under him. The child emerges holding his nose, suffering (or pretending to) from Hotei's flatulence. A hallmark of the Edo period, such bawdy humor reflects the playfulness and rebelliousness of *chōnin* patrons.

153
Okame, mid-19th century
Ivory with horn inlay; 4.8 cm
Signed: *Mitsuhiro* (1810–75, Osaka school)

The Japanese goddess of fertility, abundance, and mirth, Okame is often portrayed as a pie-faced country girl of prodigious girth and insatiable sexual appetite. The 19th-century artist Mitsuhiro conveyed her blatant sexuality here by showing her emerging from an imaginary bath and holding a round, Chinese-style fan. Her loosely held kimono immodestly falls open, revealing her breasts and soft tummy. Mitsuhiro, an expert at engraving techniques, accentuated the cherry blossoms on her robe by finely pitting the surrounding ivory to create a stippled effect.

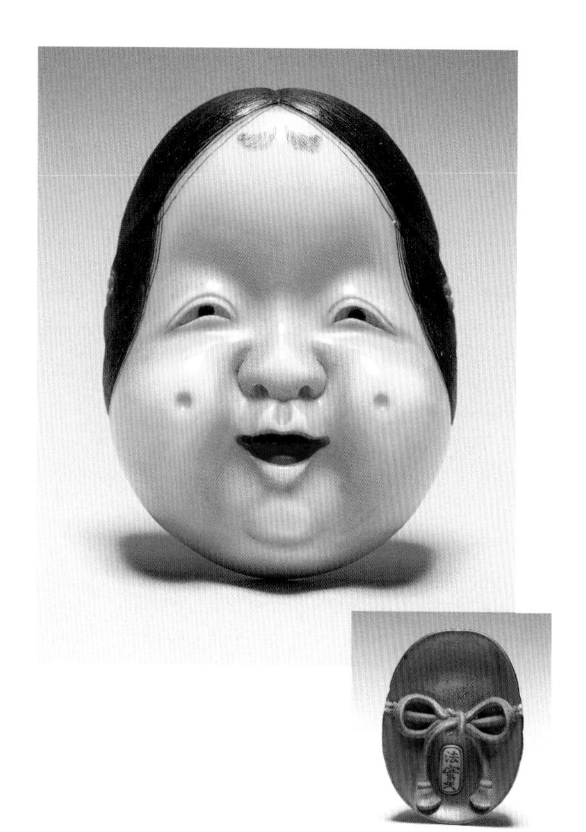

154
Okame mask, mid-19th century
Ivory and lacquer; 4 cm
Signed: *Hōjitsu* (Tokyo school)

This netsuke faithfully reproduces the type of masks used in comic Kyōgen plays to represent Okame with her fleshy, dimpled cheeks and double chin. Her eyebrows have been shaved and painted high on her forehead, a common practice among Japanese aristocrats. One of the most renowned and influential artists of the mid-19th century, Hōjitsu made finely crafted netsuke in both ivory and wood, which he embellished in innovative ways. Here, he finished the back of the mask with gold lacquer and rendered its thickly braided cord in minute detail.

155

Demon with lantern, mid-19th century
Coral; 8.5 cm
Signed: *Kōkoku* (1830–67, Tokyo school)

Netsuke artists were undoubtedly influenced by ancient Buddhist sculptures. Professional Buddhist sculptors probably also carved some of the earliest netsuke. In the 13th century, the sculptor Kōben created a pair of demonic lantern holders, standing nearly three feet high, that are still on display at Kōfukuji temple in Nara. The artist Kōkoku, who made this netsuke, must have seen Kōben's work or something derived from it. The natural color variations of the dark coral (*umimatsu*) accentuate the demon's grotesque nature.

156

Demon during *Setsubun*, mid-19th century
Boxwood; 4.5 cm
Signed: *Sukenaga* (Matsuda Sukenaga, 1800–1871, Hida-Takayama school)

In the days before a new lunar year, the Japanese stage ceremonies to exorcise demons. Chanting "*Oni wa soto, fuku wa uchi*" (Out with demons, in with luck), they throw dried beans throughout their houses to chase away any lingering evil. This netsuke shows a demon taking refuge under a sedge hat as the beans rain down. Sukenaga's attention to detail gives the work a convincing realism. The hat, for example, has signs of wear and tears under the pressure of the demon's claws. Even more surprising, however, the demon's pants have an opening that reveals female genitalia, making this an extremely unique and risqué netsuke design.

157

Batōki and the dead doctor, mid-19th century
Wood; 3 cm
Signed: *Miwa* (Tokyo school)

According to Buddhist scripture, the King of Hell determines how sinners will be punished for their earthly misdeeds. His harsh judgments are carried out by ferocious fiends, including the horse-headed demon Batōki. In a humorous reversal, this netsuke shows an ailing Batōki having his pulse taken by a dead doctor. The image here also plays on the common Japanese expression "*oni no kakuran*" (demon suffering from sunstroke), which is used to describe the unusual illness of a person who is ordinarily very healthy. The piece bears the signature of Miwa, a name used by several netsuke artists in Tokyo during the late 18th and 19th centuries. The skillful carving, small size, original theme, and naturalistic depictions of this miniature all indicate a mid-19th century date.

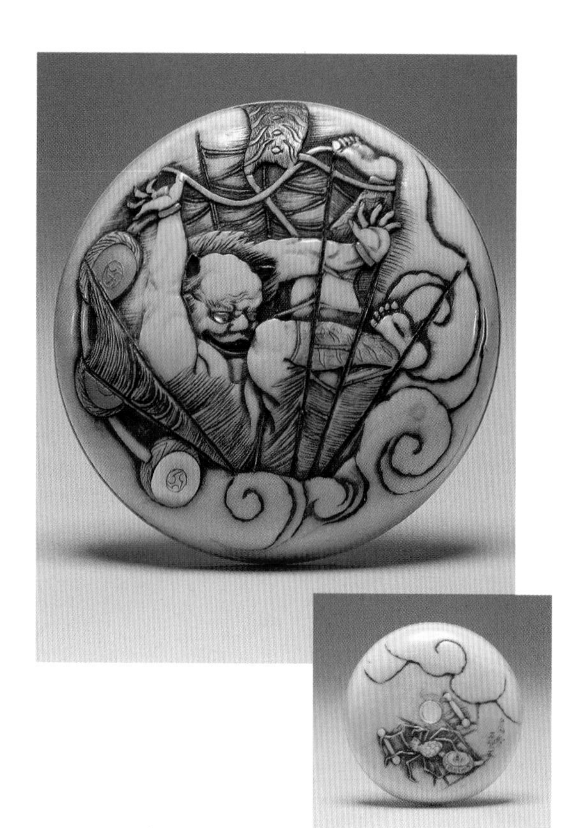

158

***Manjū* netsuke depicting the god of thunder**,
mid-19th century
Ivory with mother-of-pearl and metal inlay; 5 cm
Signed: *Hakuunsai* (Tokyo school)

Traditionally, Japanese artists depicted the gods of wind and thunder as seminaked, heavily muscled demons with bulging eyes and flamelike hair. The god of thunder generally holds two rods, which he uses to strike several drums that revolve around him. During the Edo period, however, artists tended to make the twin gods more human and often showed them suffering from various misfortunes. This *manjū* netsuke portrays the god of thunder caught in a spider's web. Adding insult to injury, he has also lost his tiger-skin loincloth. The reverse pictures the spider with more of his trophies: one of the god's drums and a pair of his mallets. The object was signed by the Tokyo artist Hakuunsai, a member of the Kikugawa family of carvers who mainly produced mask and *manjū*-shaped netsuke.

159

Ashinaga, mid-19th century
Fruitwood, coral, and ivory; 13.5 cm
Signed: *Sukenaga* (Matsuda Sukenaga, 1800–1871, Hida-Takayama school)

According to Chinese mythology, a long-legged race (Ashinaga) and a long-armed one (Tenaga) live along China's Eastern Sea. In the spirit of peaceful coexistence, they help each other fish: the Ashinaga carry the Tenaga on their shoulders into the ocean, where they snatch food from the deep water and then share it. This netsuke is unusual in showing an Ashinaga without a Tenaga. He looks into the distance and scratches his head, showing his bewilderment. He also holds a small gong, which he presumably has struck to summon his friend. Sukenaga's carving skills are evident in the superbly rendered wooden figure and his basket. Elements like the piece of coral and ivory-lined *himotoshi*, however, are more often seen in works by Tokyo school artists. But according to Sukenaga's own diary, he traveled to Tokyo in 1840, where he remained for four months. Quite possibly, he was influenced by netsuke carvers he encountered there.

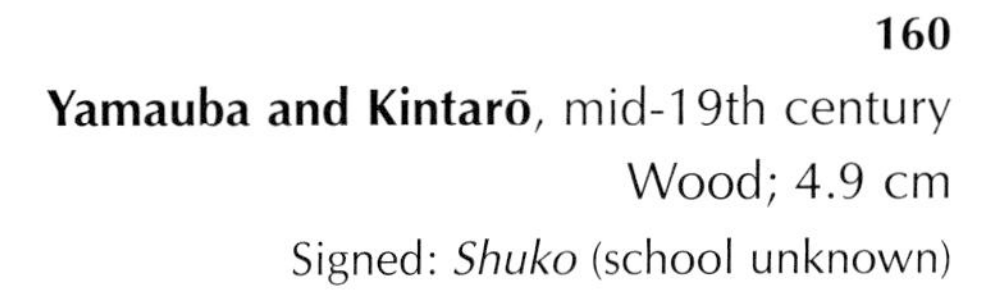

160

Yamauba and Kintarō, mid-19th century
Wood; 4.9 cm
Signed: *Shuko* (school unknown)

A popular hero in Japanese folklore, Kintarō was the child of Yamauba, a wild mountain witch. Generally, artists picture Kintarō as a handsome youth, often accompanied by the animals that befriended him in the forest. But this netsuke is unique in its intimate portrayal of the boy with his mother. Yamauba offers her son her breast, while he tugs at her sleeve. Her homely features, loose hair, bare feet, and leaf apron all betray her wild nature. Kintarō, too, with no clothes and long hair, appears equally unkempt.

161

***Namanari* mask**, mid-19th century
Wood; 5.9 cm
Unsigned

Namanari masks are used in Nō plays to portray the vengeful spirit of a jealous or scorned woman. The small horns, slight fangs, and enlarged eyes seen here suggest the beginning of the woman's transformation into a *hannya*, a female demon. This netsuke faithfully reproduces a full-scale mask in miniature, except that an actual Nō mask would have been painted.

162

Sōjōbō mask, mid-19th century
Root wood with horn inlay and cord; 8.3 cm
Unsigned

Magical mountain goblins, *tengu* have the bodies of men and the heads and wings of birds. According to legend, the oldest and greatest *tengu*, Sōjōbō, taught the martial arts to the famous 12th-century warrior Yoshitsune. Artists usually portrayed Sōjōbō with exaggerated facial expressions and the small lacquered hat of a court noble. This netsuke's maker skillfully used the twisted wooden root to convey Sōjōbō's grotesque visage and long nose. He wears a small cap associated with *yamabushi*, itinerant Buddhist priests who venerate mountains.

163

Mask cluster, mid-19th century

Ivory; 4 cm

Signed: *Hakuunsai* (Tokyo school)

During the mid-19th century in Tokyo, two netsuke makers from the Kikugawa family of carvers used the art name Hakuunsai. One of these artists seems to have specialized in mask netsuke. This work, in the *ryūsa* style, represents a jumble of masks used in Nō and Kyōgen performances. As such, it might have been commissioned to commemorate a specific play.

164

***Hyottoko* mask**, mid-19th century

Lacquered wood; 5.5 cm

Unsigned

Used in comic Kyōgen plays, *hyottoko* masks represent perplexed peasants or farmers. Such masks always feature an extremely puckered mouth and sometimes, one squinting eye. These characteristics capture the exaggerated expressions associated with unrefined people. The artist of this netsuke created a more woeful face by giving the mask large, drooping eyes. Long years of handling have worn away the thin lacquer coating, exposing the wood underneath and accentuating the mask's comical features.

165

Chinese child, mid-19th century
Wood with inlay; 4.5 cm
Signed: *Hōjitsu* (Tokyo school)

Chinese artists frequently showed children playing in gardens to symbolize happiness, procreation, and the continuation of the family line. The Japanese also delighted in this subject and faithfully reproduced the clothing and topknots worn by Chinese boys. The netsuke artist Hōjitsu favored the theme as well, varying each of his designs and embellishing them with inlays. For this netsuke, he depicted a smiling child carrying a bucket on his back.

166

Bearded man mask, mid-19th century
Ebony; 7.2 cm
Signed: *Gyokuseki* (school unknown)

This mask of a laughing old man with "smiling" eyes might be a creative interpretation of the *Kokushikijō* masks used in Nō plays to represent benevolent gods. Their black color symbolizes the earth and night. The artist here capitalized on the natural color variations of the ebony to produce a dramatic highlight along the mask's right side.

167

Tanuki* priest with *mokugyo, mid-19th century
Stag antler; 3.8 cm
Signed: *Masayuki* (Asakusa school, Tokyo)

The Japanese believe that *tanuki*, nocturnal raccoonlike dogs, possess supernatural powers, including the ability to change their shape. This netsuke portrays a rather benign *tanuki* in the guise of a Buddhist priest. Having fallen asleep, the creature leans peacefully on a *mokugyo*, a wooden bell used to keep time during chanting. Masayuki fashioned the work from the coronet of a deer antler, a section often discarded by carvers because of its irregular form. But Masayuki cleverly incorporated its flaring shape into his design to suggest the priest's widespread robes.

168

***Kappa* with frog on a lotus leaf**, mid-19th century
Ivory; 2.7 cm
Signed: *Rensai* (active 1830–80, Asakusa school, Tokyo)

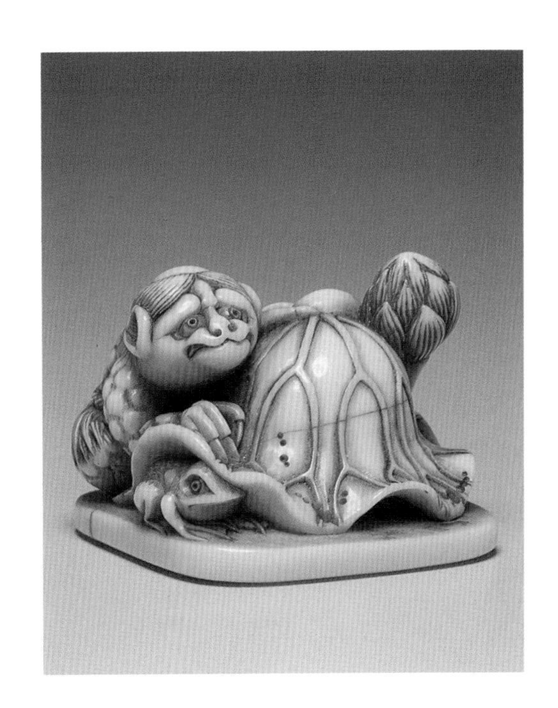

This imaginary water sprite, or *kappa*, appears more fretful than vicious as it cowers behind a lotus leaf with a frog. The artist also made the creature more human by dispensing with the turtle's carapace and giving it a fisherman's skirt and rope belt. Rensai created several designs that included rectilinear bases, recalling netsuke that doubled as seals. His works always exhibit a well-delineated precision, seen here in the veins of the lotus leaf and its minutely drilled holes, which suggest insect damage.

169

***Manjū* netsuke with animals of the zodiac,**
mid-19th century
Ivory; 4.2 cm
Signed: *Kaigyokusai* (1813–92, Osaka school)

The Osaka school artist Kaigyokusai was one of the most famous netsuke makers of the 19th century, if not of all time. Self-taught, he had a near maniacal fascination with precise and minute detail. While the idea of combining all twelve animals of the zodiac on one netsuke was not new, he challenged himself in this piece by using the demanding style of *ryūsa* openwork. Moreover, to further enliven the surface, he carved each animal as if it were running. To integrate his signature into the overall design, he suspended a narrow poem card with his name from a branch of maple leaves. Thoroughgoing to a fault, he also fashioned the *himotoshi* to resemble chrysanthemums.

170

Rat, mid-19th century
Porcelain; 5.5 cm
Unsigned

During the 19th century when netsuke production was at its height, Japanese collectors sought out novel examples, encouraging carvers to experiment with a wide range of materials. Some netsuke, like this rat, were even fashioned out of clay. While such artists as Ritsuo, Kenzan, and Kenya are associated with ceramic netsuke, it also seems likely that potters at the Hirado, Imari, and Arita workshops in Kyūshū made porcelain netsuke as demand warranted. The elegant simplicity of this miniature would have been quite striking in an era when artists crafted increasingly complex, detailed, and colorful netsuke.

171

Lucky symbols and rats, mid-19th century
Walrus ivory and gold; 4 cm
Signed: *Hakusai* (Asakusa school, Tokyo)

Using the difficult *ryūsa* style of carving, Hakusai excelled at creating complex designs. For this netsuke, he depicted a jumble of *takaramono*, or treasures, a group of ten or more objects symbolic of health, wealth, and happiness. The front of the work shows the hat of invisibility (*kakuregasa*), a key (to a treasure house), a purse, a mallet, rhinoceros horns, a scroll, and coral. The back pictures a coin, a jewel, a clove, and a jar with more coral. The cloak of invisibility and a feathered robe wrap around the sides. And among the treasures, Hakusai inlaid three golden rats, one of which tries to pull away Daikoku's mallet. Rats, in fact, are the companions of Daikoku, a popular god of grain and abundance. Because of the prominence given to Daikoku's hammer and the rats, this netsuke was probably commissioned to commemorate the Asian year of the rat.

172

Tiger, mid-19th century
"Sesame seed" bamboo and ivory; 3.5 cm
Signed: *Sekiran* (school unknown)

While Asian artists used bamboo for relief carvings, they seldom sculpted it in the round because it was difficult finding pieces large enough and the material tended to split as it dried. This netsuke, therefore, is extremely rare and made even more so by the variety of bamboo, which gives the surface its distinctive speckled pattern. In fact, by choosing bamboo, the artist here created a clever pun on the traditional Japanese theme of tigers in bamboo. In Asian art, both tigers and bamboo symbolize strength and are usually shown withstanding fierce winds and storms. Sekiran made this tiger more forbidding by giving it large ivory eyes.

173

Boar, mid-19th century

Wood; 4.7 cm

Signed: *Issan* (Iwashiro school)

Wild boar (*inoshishi*) are native to Japan, living in dense mountain forests. From ancient times, boar were hunted for sport during annual imperial expeditions. The boar's fearless charge, in fact, was infamous, and warriors who could stop an enraged animal became well known (see cat. no. 108). Interestingly, netsuke artists often chose to ignore the boar's fierce nature, depicting it sweetly asleep, perhaps on a bed of autumn foliage. Although located in the far north, artists of the Iwashiro school sometimes produced works that are remarkably similar to those by the Nagoya school in the south. Both groups created a wide range of natural subjects and gained renown for their animals' precisely rendered fur.

174

Boar, mid-19th century

Wood with inlay; 5 cm

Signed: *Ittan* (died 1877, Nagoya school)

As the twelfth animal of the zodiac, the boar often became a subject for netsuke carvers. Perhaps because of its rounded proportions, the boar also became emblematic of wealth and well-being, and people born under its sign are said to be honest, courageous, forthright, and loyal. In this skillful depiction, the Nagoya artist Ittan pitted the area beneath the animal's mouth to resemble hairy stubble. By fashioning it with its head up and forelegs out, he masterfully suggested movement, as if the great beast has just awakened and is trying to stand.

175

Rooster, mid-19th century

Wood; 4.3 cm

Signed: *Ittan* (died 1877, Nagoya school)

With its mantle of luxurious feathers, the proud and flamboyant rooster is the tenth animal of the Asian zodiac. Like other Nagoya artists, Ittan rendered this bird in a naturalistic stance rather than in the heraldic poses favored by other netsuke schools. He pitted the bird's comb to suggest its bumpy texture and carefully delineated the different feathers comprising its neck, back, wings, and tail. He then neatly tucked its clawed feet underneath its body, eliminating the problem of dangerous projections. Although this netsuke probably commemorated the year of the rooster, it might also have been commissioned by someone who enjoyed cockfighting, a popular pastime during the Edo period.

176

Hare and the moon, mid-19th century

Lacquered wood, mother-of-pearl, coral, gold, and silver pigments; 4 cm

Signed: *Hiroseki* (school unknown)

The Chinese believe that a sacred hare and a frog live on the moon and produce the elixir of immortality. However, the Japanese say that the hare-in-the-moon pounds rice in a giant mortar to make *mochi*, a sticky gluten formed into small cakes. Rounded netsuke like this are called *manjū*, after these rice cakes. Not only does the work's overall shape refer to the hare-in-the-moon, but a full moon has been included at the top with a rabbit amid autumn grasses below. The hare has been cleverly carved from mother-of-pearl to suggest luminous moonlight on its fur.

177

Monkey and crab, mid-19th century
Ivory with inlay; 3.8 cm
Signed: *Kaigyokusai* (1813–92, Osaka school)

The Japanese children's story "Saru kani kassen" (The Battle between the Monkey and the Crab) begins with the two animals fighting over a rice cake. Eventually, the crab surrenders the cake for a persimmon seed. Over time, the seed grows into a tree and bears fruit. The greedy monkey, however, steals the best fruit for himself. Seeking revenge, the crab hides an egg in the monkey's hearth. When the monkey stirs the fire, the egg explodes, burning him. When he runs out to get cold water, he is stung by a bee and slips on some seaweed. In his confusion, he then bumps into a heavy mortar, which crushes him. Thus, the monkey's downfall makes the crab believe that justice has been served. This depiction of them shows the astonishing level of Kaigyokusai's carving skills and his fondness for using the finest materials.

178

Monkey climbing bamboo, mid-19th century
Stag antler; 4.5 cm
Signed: *Masayuki* (Asakusa school, Tokyo)

The Asakusa artist Masayuki excelled at carving openwork and made netsuke from wood and the difficult medium of stag antler. For this example, he left one branch of the antler relatively intact to represent a thick trunk of bamboo. But he almost completely carved away the other branch to resemble a slender twig with leaves. In a remarkable display of skill, he added a climbing monkey that actually slides along the bamboo twig.

179

Dog's jaw and teeth, mid-19th century
Natural material; 4.7 cm
Unsigned

Early netsuke were often simple objects made from such "found" materials as pieces of driftwood or bits of coral. Although eventually eclipsed by finely carved examples, natural netsuke experienced a resurgence during the mid-19th century. Nevertheless, netsuke like this dog's jaw with teeth, which probably reflects the unorthodox tastes of its original owner, were extremely unusual.

180

***Manjū* netsuke with squirrel and grapes**,
mid-19th century
Wood; 4.5 cm
Unsigned

Chinese painters introduced the theme of squirrels foraging in grapevines during the Northern Sung dynasty (960–1126), and the subject later became popular with Korean and Japanese artists as well. This carving shows a squirrel with a luxurious tail beneath a canopy of grape leaves and spiraling tendrils. While skillfully executed, the netsuke possesses an irregular shape that must have been refreshing at a time when artists vied for ever-greater stylistic perfection.

181

Bat with young on a roof tile, mid-19th century
Wood with inlay; 3.5 cm
Signed: *Hōraku* (Kyoto school)

The Chinese regard bats as lucky creatures because the written symbol for "bat" has the same pronunciation as that for "happiness." Consequently, bats frequently occur on Chinese textiles and porcelains as auspicious images. The Kyoto artist Hōraku favored bat motifs and was known for his meticulously detailed renderings. In this design, he showed a mother bat gently sheltering a pup under her wing. By finely carving the animals' fur and using inlays for their shiny black eyes, he achieved a convincing degree of realism. In addition, Hōraku made miniatures of pavilions surrounded by trees and bridges, a theme also carved by Kagetoshi, an earlier Kyoto school artist.

182

Dove on a roof tile, mid-19th century
Ivory with inlay; 3.7 cm
Signed: *Mitsuhiro* (1810–75, Osaka school)

The Osaka netsuke artist Mitsuhiro gained fame for the understated elegance and flawless finishes of his designs. Here, he left most of the surface free from decoration and brought the lightly stained ivory to a high polish. The minutely detailed bird's wings and roof tile provide a subtle, yet effective contrast to the glossy surface.

183

Quail among millet, mid-19th century
Wood and coral; 3 cm
Signed: *Itsumin* (1830–67, Tokyo school)

The Japanese have associated quail (*uzura*) with autumn since the 13th century when the famous courtier Fujiwara Teika (1162–1241) composed twenty-four poems using birds and flowers as seasonal images. For the quail, he wrote: "'Always so alone, and now the deep grasses have withered'—/Is that what the quail is crying about amid the frosts that wait for winter?" (Kamens, trans., *Word in Flower*, p. 31). For this carving, the artist Itsumin relied on standard imagery of quail and ripened grain. The tightly huddled birds suggest the brisk air of fall and make the perfect functional shape for a netsuke.

184

Owl on tree trunk, mid-19th century
Wood with horn inlay; 4 cm
Unsigned (Nagoya school)

Although the Chinese associate owls with evil and death, Japanese poets often mention them in conjunction with autumn moonlight, and Japanese artists show them benignly sleeping on tree branches. This netsuke and catalogue number 185 follow that tradition. The artist here accentuated the bird's large nocturnal eyes with horn inlays and carefully delineated each of its feathers. He further enlivened it by having it preen its wing. In contrast to the mechanical regularity of the bird's plumage, a rotting branch has been deftly rendered, complete with insect damage and clinging vines.

185

Owl on a tree stump, mid-19th century
Wood with amber and horn inlays; 6 cm
Signed: *Ikkyū* (Nagoya school)

The large eyes and rounded body of this owl make it more comical than predatory. A smaller owl that telescopes out of a hollow in the stump enhances this playfulness. The high level of craftsmanship, however, is far from casual. The artist has precisely rendered and deeply undercut each feather and carefully inlaid the eyes with amber and horn. Ikkyū is known to have worked in both wood and ivory, although his netsuke are rare. He excelled at carving octopuses, giving them huge inlaid eyes similar to those of this owl.

186

Turtle, mid-19th century
Turtle skin and carapace; 7 cm
Unsigned

Occasionally, artists made netsuke from "found" objects. This netsuke was created from a real turtle. After carefully removing the animal's entrails and preserving its fleshy parts, the maker applied a transparent lacquer to the dried flesh for durability. He then attached a metal ring for the cord to the turtle's plastron, or underside. A renewed interest in such "found" netsuke occurred during the 19th century. The fragility of this piece, however, makes it ill-suited for actual use.

187

Snake, mid-19th century
Wood with horn inlay; 7 cm
Signed: *Totsuke* (school unknown)

Although the Japanese have many folktales about malevolent serpents, they also believe that snakes are earthly manifestations of the divine. For centuries, farmers have recognized that snakes control the proliferation of rodents and have treated with respect any snake that has taken up residence in the household's rafters. In fact, when a snake vacates the home, it is said to portend disaster. As the fifth animal of the zodiac, the snake also became a frequent subject for netsuke makers. Here, the artist rendered the reptile's long body in three loops, creating a natural *himotoshi* using a gap in its coils. He then lightly pitted the surface with a "peanut shell" technique to mimic the creature's scales.

188

Skull and snake, mid-19th century
Wood with inlay; 5.8 cm
Signed: *Sukenao* (1844–85, Hida-Takayama school)

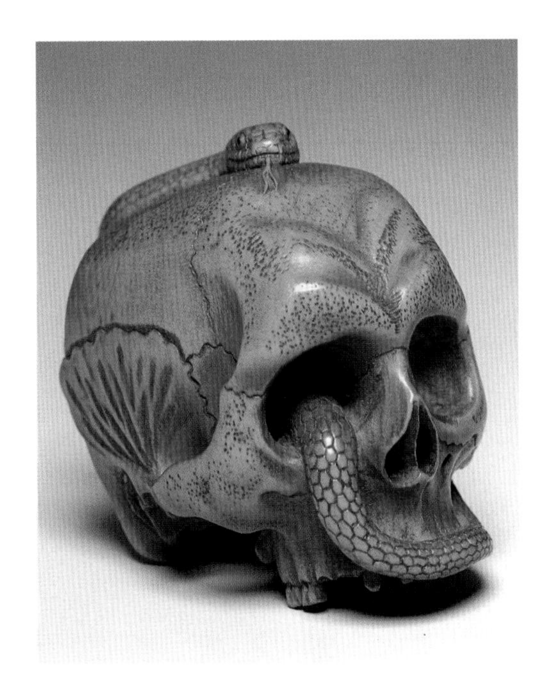

The Japanese believe that especially greedy or jealous people may be reborn as snakes after they die (De Visser, "The Snake in Japanese Superstition," pp. 303–4). This netsuke might allude to such a disastrous fate, for in it a snake slithers through the empty eye socket of a human skull. Sukenao was the leading apprentice of Sukenaga, who founded the Hida school in Takayama, and carved in a similarly precise manner as his master. He produced a number of skulls and, supposedly, his desire for accuracy was so intense he procured a corpse from a local graveyard to use as a model.

189
Three Cringing Ones, mid-19th century
Wood with metal and horn inlays; 3.8 cm
Unsigned

The Japanese refer to a snake, a toad, and a snail (or slug) shown together as *sansukumi,* the three cringing ones. They use the trio to illustrate how circumstances, or fear, contrive to limit personal freedom. The natural inclination of the snake, for example, is to eat toads. Likewise, the toad likes to eat snails. The snail, however, produces secretions that are poisonous to snakes. Thus, the snake hesitates to eat the toad, afraid that it might also ingest the toad's meal: the snail. Hence, the three creatures go hungry and live in paralyzing fear. The term *sansukumi* can also describe "the kind of deadlock that occurs in human relations when too many people get involved in negotiations" (Mirviss and Carpenter, *Wright Collection of Surimono*, p. 53). Here, the snake's crisply delineated, octagonal scales contrast effectively with the toad's bumpy skin and the slug's soft texture.

190
Three Cringing Ones, mid-19th century
Wood and horn; 4.4 cm
Signed: *Masanao* (1815–90, Yamada-Ise school)

Several artists associated with the Yamada-Ise school used the art name Masanao and specialized in making astoundingly realistic, warty toads. They also carved snakes, although less often. Regardless of subject, however, their style is unmistakable: they always arranged the scales of their serpents in the staggered pattern of brick masonry. Here, a snake holds a toad firmly in its mouth, while a slug clings to the snake.

191

Mushroom with frog and chrysanthemum, mid-19th century
Stag antler with inlay; 4.3 cm
Signed: *Rensai* (Asakusa school, Tokyo)

Rensai created a number of original designs and worked successfully in wood, ivory, and the difficult medium of stag antler. He usually made small, compact nature studies like this one. Here, he took great care to carve the delicate, radiating gills underneath the mushroom's fleshy cap. The spray of chrysanthemums hints at the coming of autumn, while the tiny, clinging frog is one of his hallmarks.

192

Clamshell with carved interior, mid-19th century
Ivory with inlay; 6 cm
Signed: *Kaigyokusai* (1813–92, Osaka school)

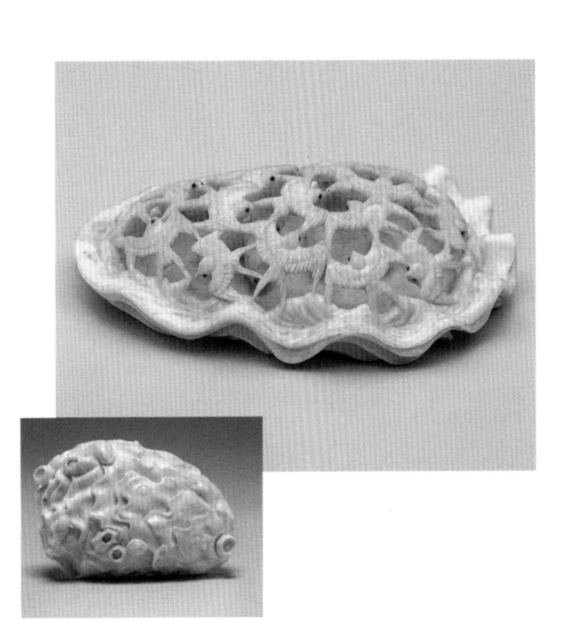

One of the most celebrated netsuke artists of all time, Kaigyokusai was famous for his consummate craftsmanship. Here, he rendered an extraordinarily detailed seashell held together by screws shaped like barnacles. The shell opens to reveal a flock of birds in flight. In an astonishing display of skill, he reticulated the entire flock, joining the birds together by the tips of their wings and tails into a canopy of carved openwork. In a final flourish, he then carved five more birds beneath the canopy, giving each inlaid eyes.

193

Octopus and abalone, mid-19th century
Wood with ceramic and metal inlays; 5.5 cm
Unsigned

Unlike earlier works that portrayed animals with human characteristics, this faithful rendition of an octopus with an abalone reveals the 19th-century Japanese interest in naturalism. Using a decorative effect employed by the Shibayama school in Tokyo, the artist embellished the work with tiny bits of inlay. He carved the underside of the abalone with stylized waves and then inlaid metallic beads to suggest sea spray.

194

Cluster of shells, mid-19th century
Porcelain with enamel overglaze; 7 cm
Unsigned

This rare porcelain netsuke of shells might have been produced to commemorate the year of the snake (see cat. no. 144). However, the work's delicate designs and overglaze enamels show the influence of decorative porcelains known as Kakiemon ware, which were made in Kyūshū starting around 1670. As such, it might have been purchased as a souvenir, marking a tourist's visit to one of the country's great porcelain-making areas.

195

Desiccated fish, mid-19th century
Fish skin, tortoiseshell, metal, ivory, lacquer, and stag antler; 6 cm
Unsigned

Generally, netsuke artists created their miniatures from pieces of wood or ivory. Occasionally, however, they used natural objects like nuts or bones. Here, an unknown artist made a netsuke from a small fish. He stretched the fish's delicate skin over a form (probably wood) and encased its head in sheets of thinly carved tortoiseshell. To represent the stringer, he attached a fine metal rope to its mouth. He also used red lacquer to represent the animal's severed body and lined the *himotoshi* with stag antler and colored ivory.

196

Snail on a cucumber, mid-19th century
Wood; 10.6 cm
Unsigned (Nagoya school)

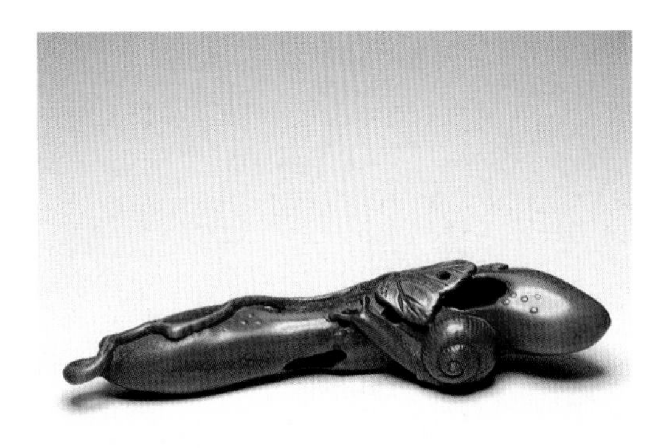

As early as the 12th century, Chinese painters started to show nature in microscopic detail and at every stage of existence. Although the Japanese, too, were fond of picturing the four seasons, they did not begin to render decaying vegetation until the Edo period, when they came under the influence of such artists as Maruyama Ōkyo, who championed Western realism. At the same time, they developed an interest in objectively depicting such creatures as insects. This netsuke of a snail traversing a cucumber graphically captures the effects of insect damage and decay. Despite the subject, the artist achieved a certain elegance through the cucumber's slender proportions and trailing tendrils. He also accurately portrayed the slick surface of the snail's shell and the bumpy texture of the snail's skin and the vegetable using the *ukibori* technique.

197

Wasp and persimmon, mid-19th century
Wood with inlay; 10.5 cm
Signed: *Kōgetsu* (Nagoya school)

Nagoya school artists often showed wasps eating decaying fruit, a common theme for the 19th century and its obsessive fascination with nature. Here, Kōgetsu varied the subject somewhat by including the persimmon's hull and broken stem. A study of textures, the work masterfully conveys the hard, cartilaginous body of the wasp with its gossamer wings and the soft, overripe fruit with its brittle skin. To not interrupt the overall design, Kōgetsu disguised the *himotoshi* as holes in the persimmon's leaves.

198

Dragonfly on a lotus leaf, mid-19th century
Stag antler with horn inlay; 5 cm
Signed: *Masayuki* (Asakusa school, Tokyo)

Both the Chinese and Japanese associate dragonflies with summer, when they hover in great numbers over streams and ponds. In this netsuke, Masayuki cleverly used an antler's irregular circumference to render a weathered lotus leaf. He also utilized the inherent imperfections of the material to suggest insect damage and probably drilled some additional holes into it to enhance that effect. For the dragonfly, he included large, orblike eyes of inlaid yellow horn.

199
Chrysanthemum, mid-19th century
Ivory; 4.5 cm
Signed: *Dōshō* (1828–84, Osaka school)

The Chinese and Japanese celebrate the ninth day of the ninth month as an auspicious occasion, marking a change of seasons. Their earliest ceremonies on that date, however, were also designed to avert illness. To that end, they drank rice wine steeped in chrysanthemum petals and bathed with cloths dampened with chrysanthemum dew. During the Edo period, they even took excursions to view exhibitions of carefully cultivated chrysanthemums. In this complex rendition, Dōshō heightened the flower's realism by reticulating several of its petals, so they appear to be unfurling. The center of the blossom, too, has been deeply carved and might have once held a plug representing the stigma.

200
Eggplants, mid-19th century
Wood; 3.7 cm
Signed: *Tadakazu* (Nagoya school)

During the summer, the Japanese harvest several types of eggplants, all of which are much smaller than Western varieties. Because eggplants contain countless seeds, they came to symbolize abundance. For this netsuke, the artist created a pile of nine round *kinchakunasu* eggplants and one long *sendai naganasu*, whose reticulated center serves as the *himotoshi*.

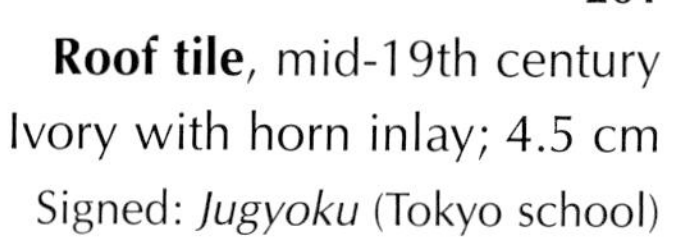

201

Roof tile, mid-19th century
Ivory with horn inlay; 4.5 cm
Signed: *Jugyoku* (Tokyo school)

Traditionally, the Japanese constructed the roofs of Buddhist temples from heavy tiles. They often molded the tiles used for the eaves in the shape of auspicious animals or symbols. This netsuke mimics the type of capping tiles placed at the ends of gables. The scowling, horned demon probably represents the god of thunder. As such, it functioned as a talisman, protecting the building against lightning. The Tokyo school artist Jugyoku worked equally well in ivory and wood, using inlays sparingly. Here, he inlaid the demon's eyes with bits of transparent horn.

202

Hobby horse, mid-19th century
Wood with horn inlay; 17.5 cm
Signed: *Masanao* (Yamada-Ise school)

To make *sashi* netsuke, artists either distorted the shapes of some objects or sought out subjects that were normally elongated, like this hobby horse. The animal here has a finely rendered mane and a carved pole resembling bamboo. It might have commemorated the year of the horse or the dance of the spring pony (*haru goma shosa*), which celebrated the new year and was performed by itinerant dancers who rode hobby horses or carried toy horse heads mounted on sticks. The netsuke has been signed "Masanao," a name used by several artists in Ise during the 19th century. They all worked in a similar style and colored their miniatures with a distinctive reddish stain.

赤穂浪

Starting in 1638, the Tokugawa shoguns endorsed a policy of isolationism that enabled them to achieve widespread stability and maintain national sovereignty. But that seclusion also prevented the Japanese from benefiting from the technological and scientific advancements of the Industrial Revolution. So when four American warships under the command of Commodore Matthew Perry entered Uraga Harbor in 1853, the shogun and his military elite could do little to stop them.

While the official reason for Perry's visit was to deliver a letter from President Millard Fillmore urging Japan to open its harbors for trade and as safe havens for foreign ships, Perry's armed presence clearly indicated that military action would follow if Japan did not comply. The "opening" of Japan the following year led to a series of inequitable commercial treaties in favor of the foreigners. That situation, coupled with chronic economic problems, eventually gave rise to strong antishogunal sentiments. Overwhelmed by these seemingly insurmountable problems, Tokugawa Yoshinobu officially resigned his position in 1867 in favor of the 16-year-old emperor Mutsuhito and, in so doing, relinquished the hereditary right of his family to rule.

Under Mutsuhito, who is better known as the Meiji emperor because of his "enlightened rule," the country embarked on a program of modernization that radically transformed it. As a way to consolidate imperial authority, Japan's feudal lords surrendered their lands to the emperor in 1871 and disbanded their private armies. In their place, a new imperial army was created through mandatory conscription. To stimulate agricultural production and thereby raise revenue, the government allowed private land ownership, which had historically been forbidden, and issued a new land-tax policy. And since it was widely accepted that the gateway to progress was knowledge, a compulsory educational system for all was established as well.

Japan moved quickly, too, to set up vital communication and transportation links. By 1871, a national and international telegraph service was in place, followed by mail service in 1872. During the 1870s, railways linking the country's major cities were built, and by 1901, one could take a train from Aomori prefecture in the far north to the port of Nagasaki in the south, with branch lines to numerous other areas. The 1870s also saw the creation of a national banking system, the founding of private banks, and the opening of the Tokyo Stock Exchange in 1878. Based on Western models, Japan's first constitution was ratified in 1889 and the first general election for seats in the House of Representatives held the following year.

In addition, the Japanese studied and adopted Western technologies for their own domestic industries. By the turn of the century, coal mining, shipbuilding, iron smelting, and steelmaking were all well established. But it was Japan's military defeat of China (Sino-Japanese War, 1894–95) and Russia

(Russo-Japanese War, 1904–5) that astonished the rest of the world and catapulted the country into the realm of powerful-nation status. While the Japanese still suffered from racially motivated Western policies, their hard-won economic and military might resulted in the abolishment of extraterritoriality in 1899, which had exempted foreigners from Japanese laws and jurisdiction. And by 1911, Japan had established tariff autonomy for itself, which permitted the raising of abnormally low tariffs on foreign imports.

During that time, in an effort to appear modern to the outside world, Japanese men started to cut off their topknots and adopt Western hairstyles. In the early 1870s, the government had its officials wear European suits rather than traditional kimonos. And in 1883, it commissioned the English architect Josiah Conder to design the *Rokumeikan*, or Deer-Cry Pavilion, a lavish European structure where foreign guests could be entertained in Western style, complete with foreign cuisine, music, and dancing. To these opulent events, Japanese men wore top hats and tailcoats, and women dressed in Victorian gowns with bustles, corsets, and petticoats.

Netsuke of astonishing sophistication and originality continued to be made in large numbers during the Meiji era.

It has often been assumed that the adoption of Western male attire during the early Meiji era quickly diminished the demand for netsuke, as pockets supplanted the need for *sagemono*. While it is true that high court officials and government employees followed the emperor's lead in wearing European clothing in 1872, there was little impetus for most men to change their traditional garb. European suits were expensive and not widely available until Japan established its own weaving and sewing industries to produce them. And even those who wore suits to work, often changed into kimonos once they returned home (Shibusawa, *Meiji Era*, p. 6). Moreover, kimonos remained the standard dress for traditional holidays and festivals.

In fact, the government's push for rapid modernization led many Japanese to realize their own culture was being lost. During the 1880s, the study of traditional Japanese art increased, and by late in the decade, a growing wave of nationalism was under way. In 1882, for example, less than seven years after it had opened, the Technical Fine Arts School for teaching Western-style painting and sculpture closed, and in 1889, the Japanese government sold the Rokumeikan. At the same time, the Tokyo School of Fine Arts and the Tokyo National University of Fine Arts and Music were founded to promote traditional Japanese culture. Nationalism also influenced fashion, and by the 1890s "a general reaction against over-Westernization led to a sort of purist approach to Japanese clothing, and when people dressed in kimonos they tended to wear or carry Japanese accessories" (Shibusawa, *Meiji Era*, p. 26). This trend undoubtedly included the wearing of *sagemono* and netsuke.

As a result, netsuke of astonishing sophistication and originality continued to be made in large numbers during the Meiji era (1868–1912). Miyazaki Josō and artists of the Sō school in Tokyo, for example, created a wide range of traditional subjects in a consistently refined style (cat. no. 206). Kyokusai, a contemporary of the early Sō school masters, produced meticulously detailed figures and nature subjects, gaining fame for his open-worked baskets and fishing nets (cat. nos. 203, 213, 217, and 218). Meanwhile, Osaka's Sanshō (cat. no. 216) and Tokyo's Tōkoku (cat. no. 219) carved sensitive portrayals of human subjects, often enlivening them with colored inlays. Shibayama school artists continued to encrust the surfaces of their netsuke with precious stones and mother-of-pearl, fashioning jewellike objects of great opulence (cat. nos. 253 and 254). And in the Asakusa area of Tokyo, the eccentric artist Kokusai used inexpensive stag antler to great effect, making powerful, stylized works (cat. nos. 230, 238, and 242) in refreshing contrast to the sometimes excessively refined designs of the established schools.

Early visitors to Japan also helped buoy the netsuke market. Charmed by these miniature "windows" onto Japanese culture, Western tourists collected old and new netsuke alike. An unusual anecdote from the time relates how a crew member on one of Perry's ships might have been the first American to acquire a netsuke:

> During the stay of Commodore Perry at Uraga, Kanagawa prefecture, in 1853, a superintendent of coolies under the Shogunate, named Mikawaya Kōzaburō, was rendering services to the visiting mission. In keeping with the fashion of the time, he wore a fine tobacco pouch with an exquisite netsuke of a stage mask. The netsuke attracted the attention of a member of the suite to the Commodore, who wished very much to have it. At his earnest request, Kōzaburō at last parted with the piece. In return the American gentleman presented the latter with things which he had brought from his country and hence were novelties in Japanese eyes. This incident was brought to the knowledge of Shogunate officials, who threw Kōzaburō into prison on the grounds that pending the negotiations between Commodore Perry and the Shogunate for opening of ports and foreign trade, it was unpardonable to barter with a foreigner before the treaty was concluded. Hearing of this, his American friend felt very sorry for him and made efforts for his release, which succeeded and Kōzaburō was set free at last (Okada, *Netsuke*, p. 32).

Some of the greatest European collections of netsuke, in fact, were formed at that time, including those of Louis Gonse, Albert Brockhaus, Frederick Meinertzhagen, Edward Gilbertson, H. Seymore Trower, and W. L. Behrens. These foreign collectors might have unwittingly precipitated changes in netsuke design among active carvers. Some designs produced during the Meiji, Taishō (1912–26), and Shōwa (1927–45) periods, for example, lack the smooth, rounded profile of earlier works that had allowed them to be easily pushed beneath the sash without snagging its fine fabric. The angular quality and projecting details of these pieces made them more dynamic and sculptural in appearance, but ultimately less functional as netsuke (cat. nos. 206, 212, 213, and 220). Possibly, the carvers, recognizing that their foreign customers did not intend to wear the netsuke, felt free to stray from practical concerns. Not coincidentally, these works are often figural and expressly Japanese in content, making them ideal souvenirs.

In turn, Japanese netsuke might have influenced some Western artists. The famous Russian goldsmith Peter Carl Fabergé, for instance, collected netsuke and emulated their compact designs in his own jewelry and sculpture.

Early European collectors also helped ensure foreign interest in netsuke through their publications. In 1905, Albert Brockhaus published *Netsuke*: *Versuch einer Geschichte der Japanischen Schnitzkunst* (An Attempted History of Japanese Carving Artistry), the first major work on Japanese netsuke to be written in a European language. Other encyclopedic publications, like Henri L. Joly's 1908 *Legend in Japanese Art* and V. F. Weber's 1923 *Kojihōten* (Dictionary of Antiquities), as well as F. M. Jonas's 1928 *Netsuke*, offered Western audiences insight into the exotic subjects and histories of the miniatures they so avidly collected.

High court officials and government employees followed the emperor's lead in wearing European clothing in 1872, but there was little impetus for most men to change their traditional garb.

203

Tekkai exhaling his soul, late 19th century

Wood; 6 cm

Signed: *Kyokusai* (Tokyo school)

The Chinese Taoist immortal Tekkai (T'ieh-kuai), literally "iron crutch," had the unusual ability to exhale his soul from his body, thus allowing it to travel freely for great distances (see cat. nos. 12 and 13). But instead of his usual crutch, this Tekkai has been given a bamboo cane. Unlike 18th-century artists who often exaggerated the physical features of such immortals for dramatic effect, Kyokusai realistically captured the wizened physiognomy of a lame, old man. He animated the figure further by showing him with inflated cheeks, about to blow out his soul. He also carefully rendered other details, like Tekkai's tattered clothing, leaf skirt, and fluttering sleeves. Kyokusai, a contemporary of Morita Sōko and Gyokusō, worked in the refined manner of the Sō school masters. Although most of his netsuke are in wood, Kyokusai was equally adept at carving ivory.

204

***Kagamibuta* netsuke with Binzuru and Kadakkabassa**, late 19th century

Ivory, gold, and *shakudō* with horn inlay; 6.7 cm

Metalwork signed: *Katsunori* (school unknown);

Ivory signed: *Hakujitsu* (school unknown)

Binzuru (Pindola) and Kadakkabassa (Kanakavatsa) are two of the sixteen original followers of Shaka (Shakyamuni), the historic Buddha. All of these holy men achieved spiritual enlightenment during their lifetimes by secluding themselves in mountain grottoes. In this netsuke, Binzuru holds a miniature stupa, a Buddhist shrine that would have housed a relic or statue of Shaka. Kadakkabassa carries a fly whisk to gently brush away insects, thus abiding by the Buddhist strictures against taking life. Rendered in repoussé, the sages appear on a panel in the shape of a scroll, representing Buddhist teachings. The surrounding ivory bowl has carved dragons, symbols of the enlightened spirit.

205

***Kagamibuta* netsuke with Shaka theme**, late 19th century
Ivory and gold; 6.4 cm
Ivory signed: *Isshōsai* (school unknown);
Goldwork signed: *Moritoshi* (school unknown)

The historic Buddha Shaka (Shakyamuni) secluded himself in the wilderness for six years and endured extreme hardships before realizing that those efforts would not lead to enlightenment. His descent from the mountains became a standard theme in Buddhist art. Typically, artists showed him with gaunt features to suggest food deprivation and with a melancholy expression to reflect his disappointment. Because of his realization, however, he is also portrayed with signs of enlightenment: the knowledge bump (*usnisa*), a circular mark on his forehead (*urna*), and a halo. Two artists collaborated to make this dramatic netsuke. Moritoshi designed the gold disk representing Shaka in repoussé, and Isshōsai carved the ivory bowl in the form of eight intertwined dragons.

206

Daikoku and Rat, late 19th century
Ivory; 4 cm
Signed: *Josō* (Miyazaki Josō, 1855–1910, Sō school, Tokyo)

An ancient Hindu deity associated with darkness and fertility, Daikoku (Mahakala) often appears in Buddhist imagery as a wrathful god with three faces and six arms. By the 8th century in China, however, he was depicted as a gentler being, who often holds a bag of treasure that he gives to the faithful. In the 15th century, the Japanese also began worshiping Daikoku as one of the Seven Gods of Good Fortune. Because the Chinese characters for Daikoku are the same as the Japanese symbols for Ōkuni, the Shinto god of agriculture, the two deities and their characteristics often became intermingled. Consequently, the Japanese often show Daikoku with bales of rice, symbols of a bountiful harvest. This netsuke pictures him pouring out the contents of a rice bale only to discover it is filled with jewels and gold pieces. His helper, a rat, holds a box used to measure rice. The work bears the signature of Josō, a pupil of the noted Tokyo master Hōjitsu. Josō eventually established his own studio, which became known as the Sō school because many of his followers incorporated the character for "sō" (from Josō) into their art names.

207

Hotei, late 19th century

Gold, *shakudō*, silver, and copper; 6.8 cm

Unsigned

An eccentric Buddhist monk, Hotei (Pu-tai) eventually became one of the Seven Gods of Good Fortune, whose original sacred characteristics were largely overshadowed by more worldly attributes. Hotei's bag, for example, was said to contain inestimable valuables, and prayers to him could supposedly bring great wealth. This opulent *kagamibuta* netsuke clearly refers to that tradition, showing Hotei with a bulging sack of treasures. These *takaramono* also adorn the bowl. This work is unusual in having been entirely made from metal, rather than the more typical combination of an ivory bowl with a metal lid. To achieve a sumptuous effect, the artist contrasted several precious metals. The gold, in particular, shines brilliantly against a background of *shakudō,* which produces a glossy, purple-black coloration.

208

Okame, late 19th century

Lacquer and ivory; 7 cm

Unsigned

The popular conception of the goddess Okame as a licentious buffoon stems from her legendary dance in front of the *amanoiwato,* the "rock door of heaven." According to Japanese creation myths, the sun goddess (Amaterasu-no-mikoto) once secluded herself in a cave, thereby depriving the universe of light. To lure her out, Okame, also known as Ame-no-Uzume, performed a lewd dance, during which her loose clothing fell off. When the sun goddess heard the other gods heartily laughing at the spectacle, she was overcome with curiosity and peeked out. The other gods seized her and pulled her out of her cave, thus bringing light back into the world again. This netsuke of Okame is remarkably conservative, showing her beautifully dressed and respectably coiffured. Her eyebrows have been shaved and placed high on her forehead in paint, like those of a fashionable noblewoman of the Heian period.

209

Karyōbinga, late 19th century
Wood; 4 cm
Undeciphered signature

According to Indian mythology, the *karyōbinga* (kalavinka) lives deep in the Himalayas and has the head and torso of a human and the body of a fantastic bird (see cat. no. 26). Its voice is said to be enchantingly melodious. Perhaps for that reason, it is believed that its song permeates the paradisaical Pure Land of Amida Buddha. Buddhist painters and sculptors rarely depicted *karyōbinga*, so their representation by netsuke artists remains inexplicable. They might have been inspired, however, by Bugaku dances, which featured fancifully costumed children playing the part of these mythical creatures. Such performances were often held at Buddhist temples and Shinto shrines.

210

Demon mask, late 19th century
Wood; 8 cm
Signed: *Toshitsugu* (school unknown)

Relatively small and delicate, most netsuke masks faithfully reproduce full-sized Nō and Kyōgen prototypes. This wooden one is unusual because of its unique design, greater scale, and powerful presence. The demon's crisply carved curls, flamelike eyebrows, and prickly skin have all been skillfully rendered. Despite his ferocious face, however, this demon nervously bites his lower lip. Since most of Toshitsugu's netsuke are of sensitively carved figures, this work might be by another artist who used the same art name.

211

Mask cluster, late 19th century
Ivory with inlay; 5.5 cm
Signed: *Shudō* (Osaka school)

Artists made netsuke in the shape of theatrical masks in great numbers. They also produced designs combining several masks in one. The artist Shudō, however, strayed considerably from those standard presentations by endowing his masks with both comical and grotesque faces. Such groupings might, in fact, relate to the popular belief in *hyakki yakō*, the night parade of one hundred demons. During the Edo period, the subject became popular with artists, who delighted in painting long handscrolls of strange apparitions that were more humorous than frightening. Shudō's cluster here includes bizarre specters with "popped" and crossed eyes, misshapen noses, and gap-toothed mouths.

212

Takebayashi Yushichi Takashige, late 19th century
Ivory with inlay; 5.1 cm
Signed: *Yasuaki* (Homei Yasuaki, Tokyo school)

The popular Kabuki play *Chūshingura* (Treasury of the Forty-seven Loyal Retainers) was based on an actual incident. In 1701, Asano Takumi-no-kami Naganori, the lord of Akō, drew his sword against his rival Kira Kozuke-no-suke Yoshinaka because of a grave insult. Since brandishing weapons at court was strictly forbidden, Asano was forced to commit ritual suicide. Asano's faithful retainers, however, vowed to avenge him despite the fact that by doing so they, too, would be sentenced to death. This netsuke depicts one of those loyal retainers, Takebayashi Yushichi Takashige, who seems to be engaged in combat in Kira's private bedchambers. Takebayashi's right foot rests on a soft round pillow; another pillow, a wooden one used by women to preserve their elaborate coiffeurs, has been thrown aside during the tussle: part of it is above his shoulder, while a drawer and a hairpin with a coral bead fall down in front of him. Like other late 19th-century carvers, Yasuaki achieved an astonishing degree of realism through his clear narrative content, anatomically correct figure, and precise detail and coloration.

213

Nasakeji, late 19th century
Wood and ivory; 3.8 cm
Signed: *Kyokusai* (Tokyo school)

In the Japanese children's story "The Tale of the Tongue-cut Sparrow," Nasakeji is a kindly old man who befriends a sparrow, whom he calls Bidori, "beautiful bird." One day, a cruel neighbor catches Bidori and cuts its tongue. When Nasakeji learns what happened, he rushes into the forest to find the sparrow. There, Bidori and other birds thank him for his many kindnesses and tell him to choose one of two boxes. The humble Nasakeji picks the smaller box and returns home. Later when he opens it, he discovers it is filled with jewels and gold coins. In this netsuke, Kyokusai masterfully conveys Nasakeji's surprise at discovering his treasure. In keeping with the late 19th-century fondness for elaborate workmanship, he skillfully combined ebony, boxwood, cherry, and ivory for marvelous effect. Moreover, like catalogue number 212, the netsuke's overt narrative content and angularity closely align it with decorative sculpture (*okimono*) of the period.

214

Urashima Tarō, late 19th century
Ivory and lacquer; 3.5 cm
Signed: *Mitsuhige* (Osaka school)

In addition to its primary function, this netsuke also served as a sake cup. The turtle, engraved fisherman, and carved box on its underside all refer to the legend of Urashima Tarō, who saved a turtle from a group of cruel boys. The next day, a beautiful woman named Otohime went to the fisherman, explaining that she was not only the daughter of the Dragon King but the turtle he had saved. Falling in love, Tarō followed her to her father's palace beneath the waves. One day, however, Tarō grew melancholy at the thought of his family. Otohime gave him a box to carry back to his home and told him not to open it. When Tarō returned to land, he discovered that three hundred years had passed and his family was gone. Confused, he opened the box and was enveloped by a strange mist, which caused him to instantly age and die. At some time, the rim of this sake cup was chipped in two places. The artist who repaired it with gold lacquer, however, cleverly expanded on the Tarō theme. To cover the smaller chip, he created a turtle. For the larger chip, he attached a piece of ivory, disguising the seam as a band of mist showing the Dragon King's underwater palace.

215

Abalone diver and octopus, late 19th century
Wood with light and dark horn inlays; 5 cm
Signed: *Masateru* (Osaka school)

In Japan, female divers have harvested abalone for centuries. Their exotic profession, plus the fact that they wore only red skirts while diving, made them the subject of numerous erotic fantasies. As early as 1798, for example, the woodblock artist Kitagawa Utamaro created a triptych of four bare-breasted divers. Later, an even more blatant Katsushika Hokusai pictured a gigantic octopus holding an enraptured diver in a sexual embrace. Soon, netsuke artists also began crafting bare-breasted divers with their multi-armed amphibious lovers. Here, Masateru comically shows a love-struck woman carrying away an amorous octopus. Masateru was the grandson of the acclaimed Osaka netsuke master Kaigyokusai. Although Masateru's works do not have his grandfather's painstaking precision, they are always well carved and imaginative.

216

Kabuki bully, late 19th century
Wood; 3.8 cm
Signed: *Sanshō* (Osaka school)

This figure's tense posture and exaggerated facial expression indicate he is performing a *mie*, a climactic moment in a Kabuki play. In all likelihood, the character is Giheiji, a cruel old man who tries to kidnap the beautiful courtesan Otatsu in the play *Natsu matsuri Naniwa kagami* (Summer Festival in Osaka). This Giheiji takes an appropriately defiant pose. The artist Sanshō worked primarily in wood, which he then lightly stained, and was known for carving figures with vivid and often distorted countenances.

217

Monkey trainer, late 19th century

Wood; 5.5 cm

Signed: *Kyokusai* (Tokyo school)

The Japanese have long considered monkeys to be lucky creatures. During the Edo period, trained monkeys were taken door-to-door at New Year's, performing tricks and giving blessings in exchange for small monetary rewards. Here, a monkey trainer beats his drum and sings, but the monkey, dressed in a jacket and cap, refuses to dance. This netsuke's somewhat bulky proportions suggest it was made early in Kyokusai's career. The finely carved and reticulated loops of the trainer's rope, however, hint at the astounding openwork that would become a hallmark of Kyokusai's style, seen especially in his nets and baskets.

218

Fisherman pulling a lobster from his net, late 19th century

Wood; 6 cm

Signed: *Kyokusai* (Tokyo school)

Kyokusai is famous for his precise and realistically carved netsuke. In this work, he aptly captured the pleased expression of a lucky fisherman. He also skillfully rendered the complicated folds of the fisherman's clothing and the minute open weave of his net.

219

Sake seller and puppy, late 19th century
Wood, ivory, stag antler, and lacquer; 5.2 cm
Signed: *Tōkoku* (Tokyo school)

Tōkoku was extremely skilled at combining several materials in a single work to achieve uncontrived naturalistic effects. For this netsuke, he used four different woods for the sake seller's garment, apron, and footwear, and ivory for his face and hands. He carved the delivery list, sake bottles, and puppy from stag antler. For contrast, he sparingly applied colored lacquer to the figure's cuffs and apron ties.

220

Courtesan with lantern, late 19th century
Ivory; 5 cm
Signed: *Ryō* (Tokyo school)

The Tokyo school artist Ryō carved finely modeled figures from top-quality ivory. Here, he expertly captured the coquettish, pigeoned-toed walk of a courtesan. Her kimono has a pattern of flying plovers, a symbol of the women of Pontochō, an entertainment district in Kyoto, and her paper lantern has an ivy crest, probably identifying her brothel. Despite the ivory's density, Ryō aptly suggested the paper lantern's lightness and fragility by delicately carving its bamboo ribs and thin handle. Because Ryō died at a young age, his production was limited, making his works extremely rare.

221

Fukusuke with drum, late 19th century

Lacquered wood with gold and mother-of-pearl; 5.5 cm

Unsigned

Fukusuke is a kind of doll representing a chubby, large-headed child. The name literally means "helping with luck" or "Luck's helper," and the dolls were thought to have talismanic power, bringing prosperity to the shopkeepers and families who displayed them. As such, Fukusuke usually wears sumptuous clothing. Here, the robes, rendered in sprinkled gold lacquer (*nashiji*), have been embellished with delicate pine boughs (symbolic of longevity) in inlaid mother-of-pearl.

222

Chinese child holding a demon mask, late 19th century

Ivory and lacquer; 5 cm

Signed: *Hōzan* (Tokyo school)

During the 19th century, netsuke artists working in Tokyo excelled at combining a variety of materials in a single work. Here, Hōzan skillfully portrayed the Chinese child's brocade garment in gold lacquer against a darkly stained wood. He carved the demon mask, as well as the child's head and hands, from ivory. The object's subtle elegance and fastidiousness show the influence of Hōjitsu, an earlier Tokyo school master.

223

Kappa, late 19th century
Wood; 6.5 cm
Unsigned

Imaginary water sprites, *kappa* have the bodies of turtles, the limbs of frogs, and the heads of monkeys or birds. The depression on the top of their heads holds a small amount of water, allowing them to briefly leave the streams and rivers where they live. Many netsuke artists represent *kappa* as glowering, evil creatures. This one is unusual because of its submissive pose and sorrowful face. The lump in its throat suggests it gobbled up something that was not entirely palatable.

224

***Kappa* carrying a cucumber**, late 19th century
Wood; 4.5 cm
Signed: *Tōun* (Tokyo school)

According to Japanese lore, the water sprites known as *kappa* loved to eat cucumbers. For a taste of such delicacies, they would venture away from their watery homes to raid nearby gardens. In this comical netsuke, a very determined *kappa* strains under the weight of a gigantic cucumber.

225

***Tanuki* teakettle**, late 19th century
Wood with black coral inlay; 2.3 cm
Signed: *Kyōsai* (school unknown)

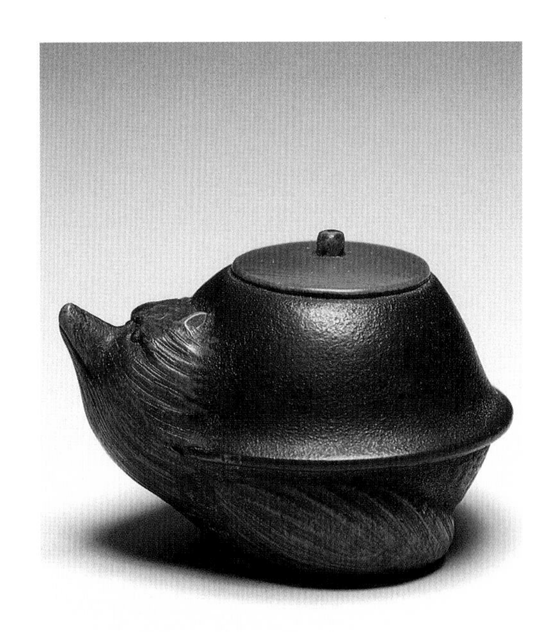

The Japanese believe that *tanuki*, racoonlike dogs native to their country, can magically change their appearance. In the children's tale "The Lucky Teakettle" (*Bumpuku chagama*), a Buddhist priest begins to heat water for tea. Suddenly, his iron kettle sprouts the head, feet, and bushy tail of a *tanuki* and begins to run around the room. After a great chase, the old priest captures the *tanuki* and puts it in a box, where it once again becomes an ordinary teakettle. This netsuke shows the *tanuki* in mid-transformation. The artist used wide, rough cuts for the animal's fur and carefully pitted and stained the kettle to suggest iron. The kettle's lid, which would have been of cast bronze, was polished smooth.

226

Twelve animals of the zodiac, late 19th century
Walnut; 3.5 cm
Signed: *Kōzan* (school unknown)

In addition to the rigors of creating miniaturized sculptures, some netsuke artists challenged themselves further by using difficult materials. Kōzan carved the hard, outer shells of walnuts to make netsuke of great intricacy and tactile appeal. In this example, he represented all twelve animals of the Asian zodiac cavorting in a pattern of stylized waves.

227

Goat, late 19th century
Wood with horn and coral inlays; 3.5 cm
Signed: *Harumitsu* (Yamada-Ise school)

Even though goats and sheep were not native to Japan, they frequently became subjects for netsuke carvers during the 19th century, probably because they were the eighth animal of the Asian zodiac. Working in the fine, naturalistic manner of other Yamada school artists, Harumitsu made functional, compact animal designs in wood. Here, he placed the goat's horns against its neck and tucked its hooves close to its body, thereby eliminating any sharp projections from the composition. He also lavished particular care on the goat's long hair and cloven hooves and animated the creature's face by inlaying its eyes with polished bits of horn and black coral.

228

Trained monkey, late 19th century
Porcelain; 6.5 cm
Unsigned

During the Edo period, trained monkeys often performed at street fairs and temple festivals. They were also taken door-to-door at New Year's, doing tricks and giving blessings for small monetary rewards. This monkey wears the formal robes and lacquered hat of a *sambosō*, an actor who performs a felicitous dance in Nō plays. The artist playfully constructed the animal with a movable head and tongue. While designs like this were produced in great numbers during the late 19th century, this one is finer than usual: smaller in scale and more delicately glazed.

229

Cat in the guise of a woman, late 19th century
Wood with lacquer; 5.8 cm
Signed: *Masaka* (1868–death date unknown, Osaka school)

The Japanese believe that cats, like foxes and *tanuki* (raccoonlike dogs), possess the supernatural ability to change shape. In this netsuke, the artist skillfully showed a cat transforming into a woman. Like alluring courtesans in woodblock prints, the creature here coyly exposes the nape of her neck. Sumptuously clothed in a kimono with a starburst pattern, this female cat needs only to make her face human to beguile men with her sensual beauty and grace.

230

***Sashi* netsuke with elephant motif**, late 19th century
Stag antler and bamboo; 15 cm
Signed: *Kokusai* (Asakusa school, Tokyo)

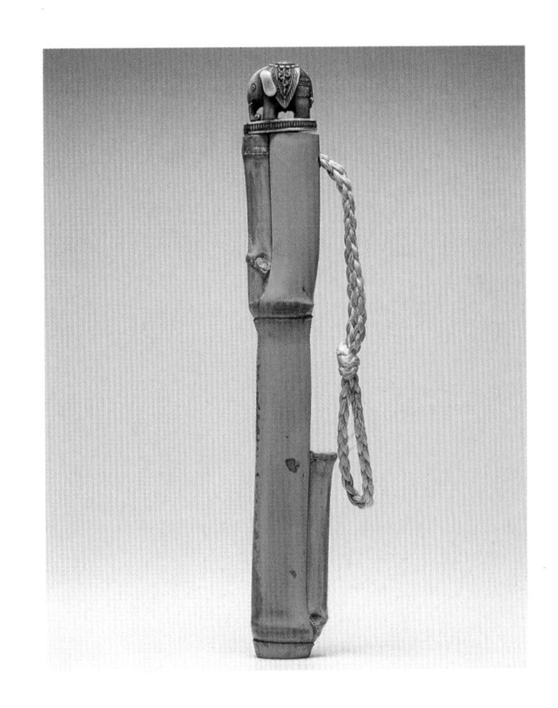

By the late 19th century, netsuke production had become increasingly repetitive, with artists copying earlier, successful designs ad nauseam. The Asakusa school artist Kokusai, however, stood out for his inventive and imaginative designs. Here, to make a *sashi* netsuke, he used a simple length of bamboo with two branches. He capped its hollow interior with a small carving of an elephant, which fits into the bamboo and includes a drilled eyelet that serves as the *himotoshi*. Elephants, in fact, were not native to Japan. A Portuguese trader took one of these exotic creatures to Tokyo in 1863, causing an immediate sensation.

231

Owl, late 19th century
Copper with silver alloy; 7 cm
Unsigned

Because of their mysterious nocturnal habits and carnivorous appetites, owls frighten the Japanese. The Chinese, too, have long believed that owls will even feast on their mothers, making them not only sinister creatures but symbols of gross ingratitude. Netsuke shaped like owls, though rare, were probably worn as talismans against rapacious behavior. This metal netsuke has been cleverly designed with an added feature: a ridged base. By striking it with a flint, this owl can light up the darkness.

232

Owl, late 19th century
Wood with ivory inlay; 5.8 cm
Attributed to Gyokumin (Tokyo school)

Artists sometimes made their netsuke with small movable parts for humorous or dramatic effect. This well-crafted owl has a tiny lever on its back that changes the bird's eyes from closed to wide open. Supposedly, its sleep has been disturbed by the children's toy depicted on its front in ivory. The toy, mounted on a dowel, consists of a small drum with two attached beads. When the dowel is rubbed between the hands, the drum revolves rapidly, causing the beads to strike the drumheads and make a loud racket. The bold simplicity of this piece contrasts with other trick netsuke from the late 19th century that were often excessively complicated.

233

Frog on pumpkin stem, late 19th century
Wood with inlay; 5 cm
Signed: *Sukesada* (1857–1920, Hida-Takayama school)

In the city of Takayama, Hida school artists specialized in carving frogs. Sukenaga, the school's founder, kept frogs as pets to observe them more easily. In this netsuke, his follower Sukesada made a frog with one outstretched leg crawling along a pumpkin stem. He skillfully rendered the frog's bumpy skin by using the *ukibori* technique, whereby textured, raised bumps are created by compressing the wood with a stylus, planing away the surrounding area, and then hydrating the surface so the compacted designs pop out.

234

Three Cringing Ones, late 19th century
Boxwood with inlay; 4 cm
Signed: *Sukeyuki* (active 1870–1900, Hida-Takayama school)

Hida school artists in Takayama liked the theme of the Three Cringing Ones, or *sansukumi* (see cat. nos. 189 and 190). In his carvings, Sukeyuki emulated netsuke of snakes by the master Sukenaga, in which openings between the animals' coils served as *himotoshi*. Unlike Sukenaga, however, who used stains of varying intensities to heighten and contrast different textures, Sukeyuki usually applied a light stain overall. Moreover, he surpassed Sukenaga in creating inlays for the creatures' eyes. He fashioned tiny glass orbs that fit perfectly into the carved eye sockets, enhancing them with painted black pupils and gold lacquered edges.

235

Talon grasping a skull, late 19th century

Bird's claw and walnut with metal attachment; 6 cm

Unsigned

Artists sometimes utilized "found" materials for their netsuke. Here, the maker used the talon of a bird-of-prey, probably a falcon. He tied the freshly severed claw in place, as if grasping a human skull, and allowed it to dry in that position. He fashioned the skull from a walnut shell. The macabre combination gives the impression of a giant winged predator dropping from the skies to carry away its terrified victim. Variations on this theme included claws clutching carved monkeys or crystal globes.

236

***Sashi* netsuke of a praying mantis**, 1868

Bamboo; 15.3 cm

Signed: *Gyokkin* (1816–80, Osaka school)

This *sashi* netsuke has a lengthy inscription on the reverse stating it was made from a piece of bamboo from Tōdaiji, an 8th-century temple built by the emperor Shomu in Nara, which continues to be one of the largest Buddhist compounds in Japan. The artist also incised the mantis's wings with two stylized Chinese characters that mean "temporary dwelling." These references probably allude to the transitoriness of life, just as the hard shell of the insect serves only as a temporary abode for the living organism.

237

Cicada on a leaf, late 19th century
Wood; 6 cm
Signed: *Harumitsu* (Yamada-Ise school)

In this masterful netsuke, the Yamada-Ise school artist Harumitsu suggested the coming of autumn. Here, an adult cicada, which only lives for a month, clings to a decaying leaf, while a spider lurks below. To suggest decomposition, Harumitsu carved the leaf with curled edges, ragged holes, and a pitted surface. He further heightened the work's visual impact by contrasting the crumbling leaf with the eerie perfection of the cicada's hard body.

238

Octopus, late 19th century
Stag antler; 10.2 cm
Attributed to Kokusai (Asakusa school, Tokyo)

An Asakusa school artist, Kokusai designed a number of amusing *obi-hasami* netsuke and might have made this example. The octopus here has comically long tentacles, which have been gathered together and stretched out. Their curling ends form the bottom hook of the *obi-hasami*, and two additional arms create the top hook. The octopus furrows its brow, seemingly aware of its ridiculous position. Such inventiveness and exaggeration were typical of Kokusai's compositions.

239

Octopus pot, late 19th century
Ceramic and lacquer; 4 cm
Signed: *Teiji* (school unknown)

This netsuke cleverly varies the theme of an octopus caught in an earthenware pot by showing the animal ensnared in a woven basket covered with clay. Like other netsuke by Teiji, the work combines unusual materials for added visual effect. The artist applied lacquer over the clay, making the octopus red against the dull black of the trap. To heighten the realism, he revealed some of the underlying basket where the clay has fallen away. The octopus, struggling to get free, frantically reaches through one of the holes.

240

***Fugu* (Globefish)**, late 19th century
Tagua nut; 4 cm
Unsigned

The artist here modified the rounded shape of a tagua nut to portray a globefish's comically distended proportions. During the late 19th century, Japanese carvers used tagua, also known as vegetable ivory, as a cheap substitute for real ivory. Although this example has been finely rendered, many inferior tagua netsuke were made at the time and sold to foreign tourists.

241

Fungus cluster, late 19th century
Wood; 4.8 cm
Signed: *Masakatsu* (1840–99, Yamada-Ise school)

The Chinese and Japanese have long believed in the pharmacological benefits of certain plants and herbs. They used dried mushrooms and fungi of all kinds for medicinal purposes. They even thought that *reishi* (*ling-chih*, or cloud-ear fungus) was powerful enough to cause immortality. For that reason, artists often show Taoist sages and Buddhist deities carrying scepters in the form of stylized *reishi*. Here, however, the artist Masakatsu realistically rendered the auspicious fungus, carefully noting its smooth stems and bumpy caps. Masakatsu was the son of Masanao (1815–90), the founder of the Yamada school in Ise. Like other artists of that school, Masakatsu specialized in nature subjects carved from boxwood.

242

***Sashi* netsuke in lotus shape**, late 19th century
Stag antler with metal; 20.3 cm
Signed: *Kokusai* (Asakusa school, Tokyo)

The Tokyo artist Kokusai excelled at carving stag antler. For this elegant netsuke, he removed the antler's spongy interior and then cut the narrow branch into a lotus bud and leaf. He skillfully used the material's porous imperfections to suggest insect damage caused by marauding ants. The ants, in fact, might have been crafted by Gambun, an artist who was famous for such minute metalwork and active in both Tokyo and Kyoto.

243

***Manjū* netsuke with flower motif**, late 19th century
Coconut shell; 4.2 cm
Signed: *Hōrai* (school unknown)

Hōrai fashioned this oval netsuke from an unusual substance—coconut shell. Because of the material's thinness and curvature, however, he needed to join three pieces together to fabricate it: a front, a back, and a narrow strip joining them. He then carved a delicate mélange of chrysanthemums on all its surfaces. The Japanese associate chrysanthemums with autumn, making this netsuke an especially suitable accessory for a fall outing to view such flowers.

244

Tea ceremony objects, late 19th century
Ivory; 4 cm
Attributed to Gyokuhō (Tokyo school)

During the 19th century, artists made netsuke shaped like clusters of objects representing their owners' favorite pastimes. Carved from a single piece of ivory, this netsuke has all the things necessary for a tea ceremony: a tea kettle, rings to lift it from the fire, a feather fan to sweep the hearth, a narrow tea scoop, and a split bamboo whisk. The artist even carefully patterned each object's surface. For example, the freshwater jar displays a ceramic crackle pattern, and the bag that holds the tea caddy, an abstract design often seen on fine Chinese brocades.

245

***Manjū* netsuke of Buddhist objects**, late 19th century
Ivory; 3.3 cm
Signed: *Hodō* (Tokyo school)

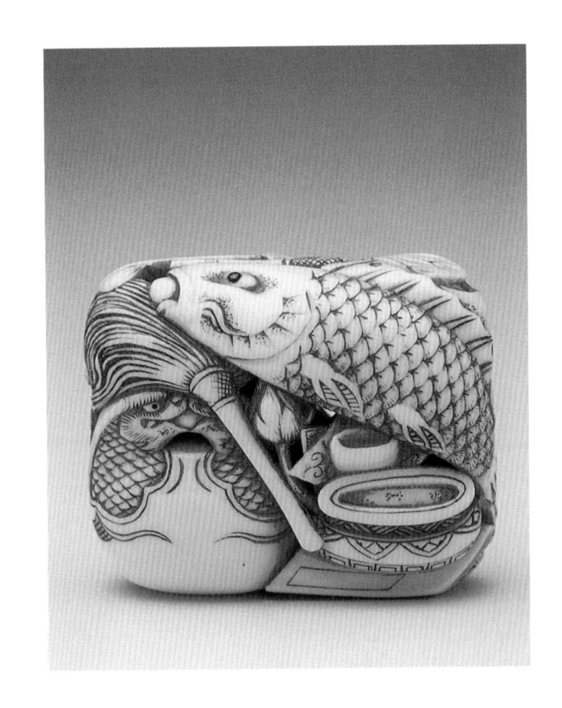

During the 19th century, artists, perhaps inspired by netsuke carved to resemble clusters of masks, began to fashion miniatures consisting of multiple objects. These groupings probably reflected the various interests and pastimes of their owners. This one features several expertly rendered Buddhist objects: a horsehair whisk, a fish-shaped sounding board, a wooden gong (*mokugyo*), a rosary, a book, and a lotus bud. Although arranged in a tight composition, the elements have been distinguished from one another by small, precise perforations.

246

Abacus, late 19th century
Persimmon wood, ivory, and brass; 4.8 cm
Unsigned

Like larger abacuses, this miniature can be used for mathematical calculations. Its small ovoid beads slide freely along their brass dowels, and the strip of ivory carries the numbers. It can also serve as a netsuke or a pendant. Holes for attaching the cord exist on the back, and one end has a small brass eyelet, allowing it to be worn around the neck.

247

***Go* board**, late 19th century

Wood, lacquer, mother-of-pearl, ivory, horn, and glass; 3.3 cm

Signed: *Sōichi* (Tokyo school)

The Chinese introduced the Japanese to *go* during the 8th century. To play the board game, participants use small white and black stones, attempting to surround the opponent's stones and thereby win. A pastime of the nobility, *go* was enjoyed by all classes of Japanese society during the Edo period. This netsuke has been carved in the shape of a *go* board; it also includes a miniature tobacco pouch and a pipe case with a blue *ojime* and a *manjū* netsuke. Together, the objects probably represent the personal indulgences of the original owner.

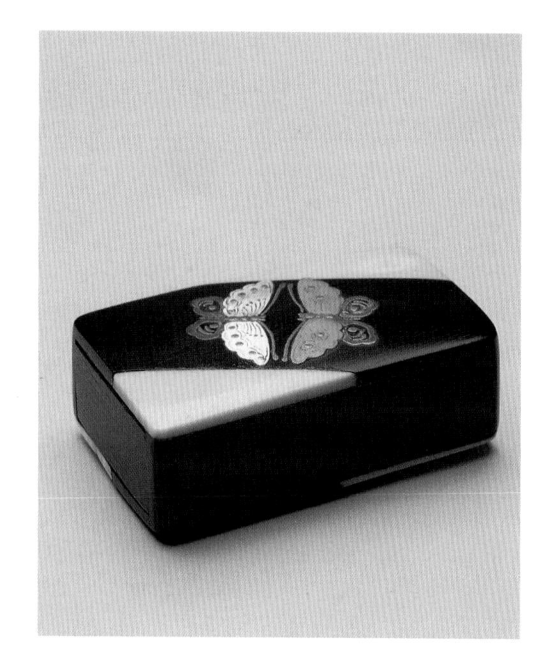

248

Box netsuke (*hako*) with butterfly pattern,

late 19th century

Marine ivory, ebony, mother-of-pearl, and gold lacquer; 4.5 cm

Unsigned

This netsuke resembles a lacquered writing box (*suzuribako*). A pair of butterflies decorates the top. Historically, both the Chinese and the Japanese associated butterflies with feminine beauty and grace. They even used the term "butterfly," or "moth," to euphemistically refer to gorgeously dressed courtesans. Paired butterflies, however, symbolized marital happiness and well-being, in part because the Chinese word for butterfly, *hu-tieh*, can also mean "double happiness" when written with different characters. This netsuke might have been made by two craftsmen: one would have constructed the box from small pieces of ebony and ivory, while the other, probably a lacquer artist, would have inlaid the butterflies using mother-of-pearl (*aogai*) and gold lacquer.

249

Storage jar, late 19th century
Metal; 3.5 cm
Undeciphered signature

During the 19th century, netsuke artists experimented with a variety of substances. Often, they used them to such unique effect that the materials are not easily identifiable. This netsuke, crafted from various metal alloys, faithfully duplicates an ordinary ceramic storage jar. Its surface, sprinkled with silver filings, resembles the rough texture of coarse clay. The jar's shoulders have been coated with *shakudō* (an alloy of gold and copper) to suggest the smooth ash glazes that naturally occur in wood-fired kilns. The cord passes through an opening on the jar's back and attaches to an eyelet on the underside of the lid. The lid itself, in copper and *shibuichi* (an alloy of copper and silver), features a swirling, cloudlike pattern.

250

Stirrup, late 19th century
Metal and lacquer; 5 cm
Unsigned

During the peaceful Edo period, samurai commissioned metal-workers to make decoratively embellished weapons that were rarely, if ever, used. On occasion, such craftsmen also produced netsuke. Here, an unknown artist carefully reproduced a metal stirrup in miniature. Like full-sized stirrups from the era, this netsuke has been lavishly ornamented. Silver cherry blossoms cover its exterior, while its interior has been lacquered a brilliant red.

251

Helmet, late 19th century

Various metal alloys and cord; 5.5 cm

Unsigned

This netsuke painstakingly replicates the details of a metal helmet. To mimic a crimped flange construction, the bowl has been ridged and then crowned with a decorative medallion. The front features a dragon's head flanked with crenolated shapes that suggest fanciful long blades. The owner's wisteria crest appears on the curved face protectors. And like actual helmets, the plates of the neck guard have been laced together with cord.

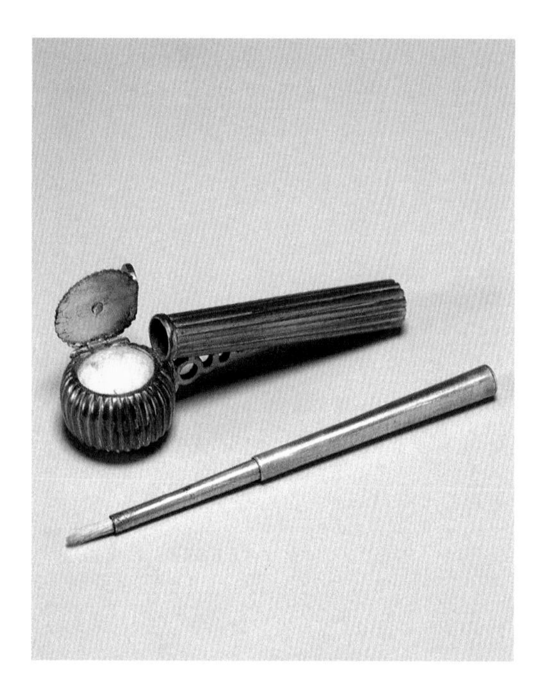

252

Miniature writing set (*yatate*), late 19th century

Silver and copper; 6 cm

Unsigned

Small, portable writing sets were probably first designed for warriors on military campaigns. By the Edo period, they had become a practical and fashionable accessory for all levels of Japanese society, who took them on seasonal outings to the countryside to view nature and write poems describing its beauty. This writing set is even smaller than usual, allowing it to also function as a netsuke. The brush has a telescoping handle and fits neatly into the case. The lidded bowl can hold a small cake of dried ink.

253

Umbrella, late 19th century

Ivory with wood, horn, metal, lacquer, and mother-of-pearl; 8.5 cm

Signed: *Shibayama* (Tokyo school)

Umbrellas and parasols were originally prestige items, shielding high-ranking aristocrats from the sun and the rain. During the Edo period, however, they were used by all classes of Japanese society. This netsuke represents a type of heavily oiled paper umbrella that became popular during the 17th century. It featured a bold circular pattern known as *janome*, or "snake's eye." This one also includes a delicate willow branch and a small bird, allusions to women. The three elements together probably refer to the beautiful courtesans of the pleasure quarters, who often went on strolls with their parasols. Shibayama, literally "grassy mountains," was the art name of Onogi Senzo, an 18th-century Tokyo artist who embellished his works with a variety of refined, semiprecious inlays. Carvers who employed this technique, including the maker of this netsuke, also used the same signature.

254

Double elephant-headed urn with lion lid, late 19th century

Wood with mother-of-pearl, coral, ivory, lacquer, and malachite inlays; 5.5 cm

Signed: *Shibayama* (Tokyo school)

Followers of the late 18th-century netsuke carver Shibayama Senzō embellished their works with extensive inlays of semiprecious materials. This fanciful 19th-century netsuke replicates the bronze incense burners placed on Buddhist altars. Most netsuke in the Shibayama style tend to be garishly inlaid. This one, however, has elegant ornamentation and excellent carving.

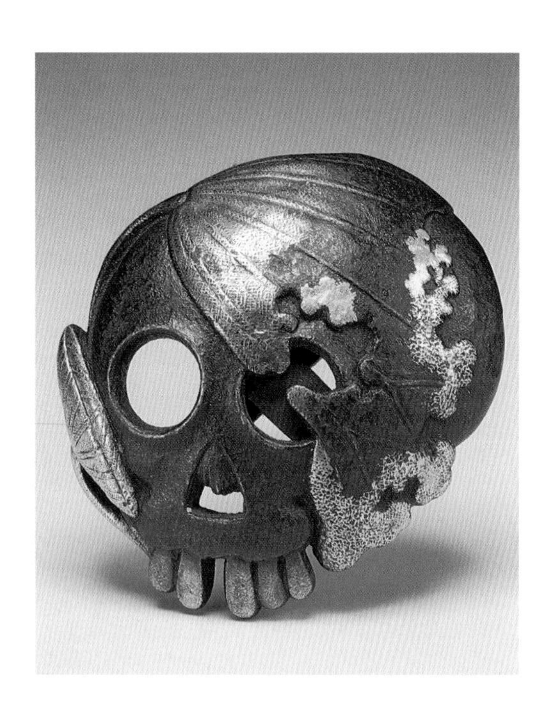

255

Skull, late 19th century

Iron with gold and silver; 4.3 cm

Signed: *Ryūshinshi* (school unknown)

The eccentric Japanese priest Ikkyū (1394–1481) once mounted a human skull on the end of a bamboo pole and paraded it through the streets on New Year's Day. His strange behavior reminded people of their own inevitable demise and encouraged them to attend to their spiritual salvation. For the same reason, skulls became a frequent theme for Zen painters during the Edo period. This rendition of a human skull adheres to that tradition. The lotus, rendered in gold, signifies spiritual rebirth, while the tattered leaf, in iron with gilded edges, suggests decay. Ryūshinshi cleverly placed a bone beneath the skull, thereby forming a discreet *himotoshi*.

During the Taishō era (1912–26) and the decades preceding World War II, Japanese workers increasingly abandoned farming and other traditional occupations for jobs in factories. At the same time, the country's successful military campaigns against China and Russia encouraged further colonial ambitions, and an increasing number of men enlisted in the imperial army. Since both factory workers and soldiers wore uniforms, Western dress became increasingly common for Japanese men. And as pockets replaced the need for *sagemono,* demand for netsuke gradually decreased. Finally, World War II and the crippling poverty of its aftermath delivered a devastating blow to the netsuke trade.

A number of artists who had been trained before the war, however, returned to netsuke carving in the late 1940s despite the fact that, by then, the art form had become quite outmoded and not very lucrative. These artists included Sōsui, Masatoshi, Ryūshi, Ichiro, and Shoko, who all represented the grand tradition of netsuke carving, each having been schooled under a noted master with an established lineage. Their commitment to maintaining the high standards of the past meant that they lavished considerable time on each netsuke and therefore produced relatively few pieces every year. Given the financial constraints of postwar Japan, they seldom received adequate compensation for their hard work. But because of their devotion to the art form, often at great personal sacrifice, netsuke carving remained viable into the mid-20th century.

Several other factors contributed to the survival and eventual resurgence of netsuke production. Interest among foreign collectors, which began immediately after the 1868 opening of Japan, continued unabated after World War II. As impoverished Japanese families sold portions of their collections to raise money, outsiders benefited from being able to buy very fine, historic pieces at low prices. Meanwhile, in Europe and the United States, the availability of reasonably priced netsuke through antique dealers and auction houses fostered a burgeoning population of enthusiastic collectors.

Unlike their 19th-century predecessors, these collectors had the added advantage of a growing library of netsuke literature. A reprinting of F. M. Jonas's 1928 book on netsuke, for instance, appeared in 1960, and Raymond Bushell translated Ueda Reikichi's 1943 *Netsuke no kenkyū* (A Study of Netsuke) into English in 1961. Then, an English version of Albert Brockhaus's 1905 classic, *Netsukes,* was released in 1969. During the 1970s, Bushell's *Collectors' Netsuke* and Betty and Melvin Jahss's *Inro and Other Miniature Forms of Japanese Lacquer Art* were published, as well as Bernard Hurtig's *Masterpieces of Netsuke Art,* Neil Davey's *Netsuke,* George Lazarnick's *Signature Book of Netsuke, Inro and Ojime Artists in Photographs,* and Marie-Thérèse Coullery and Martin Newstead's book about the Baur collection. In 1981, Lazarnick's opus was updated and reissued in two volumes as *Netsuke and Inro Artists and How to Read Their Signatures.*

Also by the mid-1970s, study associations began to be formed in the West. The International Netsuke Collector's Society hosted its first convention in 1975 in Honolulu. In the same year, the Midwest Netsuke Collectors Society met for the first time in Kansas City, Missouri. In 1977, the Midwest society changed its name to Netsuke Kenkyūkai (Association for the Study of Netsuke) and then to the International Netsuke Society (INS) in 1995 to better reflect the growing diversity of its membership. It also published a newsletter, which grew into a full-fledged journal in 1981. Today, the INS has chapters in New York, Chicago, Cleveland, Washington, D.C., San Francisco, Los Angeles, and Tokyo. Netsuke enthusiasts founded a European chapter in London in 1991 and began to publish their own bulletin in 1995.

While drawing inspiration from the grand traditions of netsuke carving, contemporary artists bring fresh ideas, unusual techniques, and new and interesting materials to netsuke production.

Exhibitions at major American and European museums, too, helped validate netsuke as an important art form. In 1976, for example, the British Museum displayed more than four hundred netsuke, followed by exhibitions at the Newark Museum (1976), the Nelson-Atkins Museum of Art in Kansas City (1977), the Yale University Art Gallery (1979), and the Los Angeles County Museum of Art (1981).

While most foreign collectors depended on art dealers and auction houses as suppliers of netsuke, a few began to commission works directly from contemporary carvers. Shortly after the war, for instance, Raymond Bushell patronized Masatoshi and Sōsui. Later, Bernard Hurtig developed close relationships with such younger carvers as Kangyoku, Bishū, Hideyuki, and Meikei. Miriam Kinsey's 1977 book, *Contemporary Netsuke,* also did much to heighten awareness about living netsuke artists among Western collectors.

By the 1960s and 1970s, Japan's postwar recovery was well underway, and interest in netsuke, both old and new, had begun to reemerge domestically. Baron Seinosuke Gō's superlative collection of netsuke and inrō, which he gave to the Imperial Household Museum (now the Tokyo National Museum) in 1942, was first exhibited in its entirety in Japan in 1959 and again in 1975. Starting in 1978, selections from that collection were also shown annually at exhibitions sponsored by the Nihon Zōge Chōkoku Kai (Japan Ivory Carving Association). Around the same time, the Nihon Netsuke Kenkyūkai (Japan Association for the Study of Netsuke) was founded and began to publish a journal in 1977. In 1983, Seibu department store began to host annual exhibitions of contemporary netsuke as well. More recently, the involvement of such high-profile personalities as Prince Norihito Takamado has further encouraged the collecting of netsuke. In fact, during an address to the International Netsuke Society in 1991,

Takamado jokingly remarked that he had caught the netsuke "disease" from his wife, Princess Hisako, who had begun a collection while still a student.

Because of this widespread awareness and popularity, netsuke also have started to be made by non-Japanese carvers, whose assiduous knowledge of Asian examples and techniques, coupled with their own creativity, has resulted in objects of astounding beauty and great depth. For some, the high quality of their work has led to honorary memberships in Japanese carving associations and inclusions in special exhibitions. In the British Museum's recent exhibit of contemporary netsuke, for example, fourteen artists out of fifty were non-Japanese. And this catalogue includes works by the English artists Michael Birch, Nick Lamb, Guy Shaw, and Michael Webb; the Americans David Carlin, Janel Jacobson, Armin Müller, and Jim Kelso; and the Australian Susan Wraight.

While drawing inspiration from the grand traditions of netsuke carving, contemporary artists bring fresh ideas, unusual techniques, and new and interesting materials to netsuke production. And since netsuke are now rarely worn, these makers have been freed from the limitations of function to explore the medium in countless, exciting ways. As a result, netsuke carving, which began nearly four hundred years ago, continues to flourish today with remarkable ingenuity and spirit.

256

Handaka and dragon, 20th century
Wood with horn inlay; 8.5 cm
Signed: *Akihide* (born 1934)

The supernatural nature of the Buddhist holy man Handaka is usually suggested by his companion, a dragon. The Japanese artist Akihide stopped making the Handaka on the left when he realized it looked like his head was being gouged by the dragon. After reevaluating the composition, Akihide carved a new design with the dragon's foot resting on Handaka's shoulder, as seen in the finished netsuke on the right. Akihide apprenticed with his uncle, a carver of decorative sculpture (*okimono*), for seven years before working in a commercial shop. Since 1974, he has been an independent netsuke carver. He has gained admiration for his creative interpretations of traditional subjects, as well as for his fine tortoiseshell inlays, which he skillfully uses to depict the bodies of insects and the carapaces of turtles and *kappa* (Kinsey, *Living Masters of Netsuke*, pp. 59–64).

257

Daruma, early 20th century
Wood with inlay; 3.8 cm
Signed: *Ryosai* (Ryosai Eguro, 1881–1949, Hida-Takayama school)

Japanese artists frequently portrayed Daruma (Bodhidharma), the Indian sage whose legs atrophied and withered away after nine years of seated meditation in China's Shaolin-ssu temple. Because of that legend, Japanese children's toys of the sage are often shaped like eggs and weighted to right themselves when pushed over. This netsuke echoes the form of such toys, but Daruma's expression vividly captures the physical anguish he endured to attain enlightenment. The artist here, however, also added several metaphorical elements to his depiction. The sage's right thumb, for example, penetrates the space between his index and middle fingers, which is a Japanese gesture referring to sex. In addition, Daruma's robes have been decorated with *noshi* and pearls. *Noshi*, strips of dried abalone tied in a knot, represent the conjugal joining of a man and woman, and magic pearls are used by Buddhist deities to grant wishes. Consequently, this netsuke suggests that Daruma's pain is not from prolonged sitting, but from abstinence, and his true wish is not for enlightenment, but for sex.

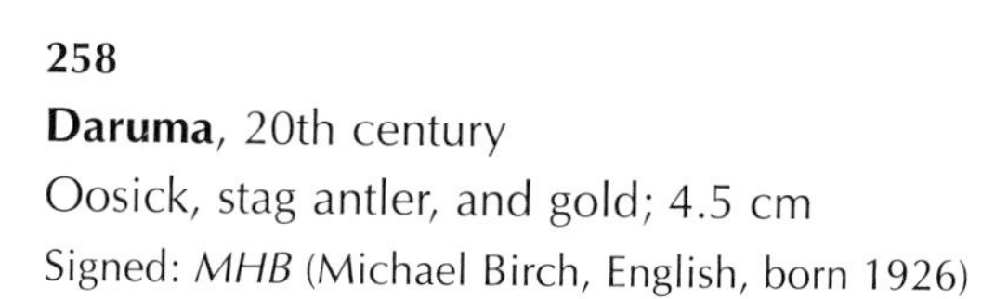

258

Daruma, 20th century

Oosick, stag antler, and gold; 4.5 cm

Signed: *MHB* (Michael Birch, English, born 1926)

For this work, Michael Birch followed tradition by showing Daruma (Bodhidharma) as a legless, egg-shaped children's toy. But he made the netsuke from a most unusual substance—oosick, dried walrus penis. He carved the material's speckled exterior to resemble the figure's robe and used the white interior for the sage's face. Birch, who now lives in England, was born in Egypt and raised in France. In his early twenties, he began carving netsuke from discarded billiard balls. He trained himself by closely studying Japanese netsuke he owned. Early in his career, he derived his subjects from Chinese and Japanese mythology, but more recently has drawn inspiration from pre-Columbian, Native American, Egyptian, and modern sculpture. In turn, his elegant, abstract compositions may have influenced Japanese makers to experiment with more contemporary forms and materials (Kinsey, *Living Masters of Netsuke*, pp. 151–60).

259

Watanabe-no-Tsuna and Ibaraki, 20th century

Ivory with coral inlay; 5 cm

Signed: *Keiun* (1912–88)

According to legend, the female demon Ibaraki terrorized people who tried to pass through Kyoto's Rashōmon gate. The Japanese warrior Watanabe-no-Tsuna (953–1024) went to kill her, but became distracted by a beautiful woman. As they rode away together on his horse, he glanced over his shoulder and was horrified to discover that she was really Ibaraki in disguise. He quickly drew his sword, but only managed to cut off her forearm before she escaped. Watanabe presented the severed limb to his master, Minamoto-no-Raikō, who locked it away in a casket. After six days, Raikō's old aunt visited him and begged to see his "trophy." When he opened the box, she grabbed the arm and fled, transforming back into Ibaraki. Here, we see the very moment when Watanabe cuts off her arm, which falls from her sleeve to the ground. The netsuke's maker, Keiun, was born in Kyoto but lived and worked in Uji. Self-taught, he was greatly influenced by Kaigyokusai (see cat. nos. 169, 177, and 192), especially by the 19th-century master's meticulous craftsmanship and attention to detail. Keiun's most famous subject portrays the cleaning of the colossal Buddha in Nara, which shows tiny figures climbing over the statue and standing on miniature ladders.

260

Miminashi Hoichi, 20th century
Wood; 6 cm
Signed: *Meikei* (Takayama Seisho, born 1932)

The contemporary Japanese artist Meikei specializes in carving heroes and legendary characters, some of whom are so esoteric they have never been depicted before in netsuke form. The figure here was a famous chanter and storyteller. One night, the ghost of a dead Taira warrior appeared before Hoichi and demanded that he recount the history of the 12th-century wars between the Taira and Minamoto families. Hoichi realized that the apparition would kill him at the end of the tale. So for protection, he asked a priest to write Buddhist scriptures all over his body, but the priest inadvertently forgot Hoichi's ears. When Hoichi finished the tale on the third night, the Taira ghost tried to kill him, but only succeeded in tearing off his ears. Meikei studied with Meigyokusai for almost twenty-five years and did not become an independent carver until 1975. Initially, he worked almost exclusively in ivory, but later became enthralled with wood for its natural richness and warmth (Kinsey, *Living Masters of Netsuke*, pp. 113–22).

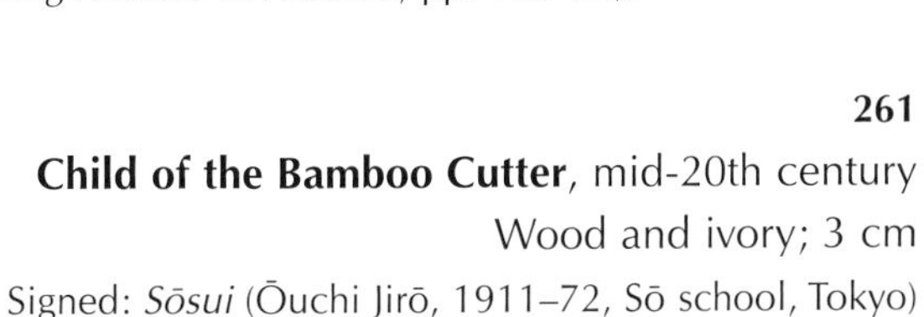

261

Child of the Bamboo Cutter, mid-20th century
Wood and ivory; 3 cm
Signed: *Sōsui* (Ōuchi Jirō, 1911–72, Sō school, Tokyo)

In the classic Japanese "Tale of the Bamboo Cutter" (*Taketori monogatari*), a moon princess is forced to live on earth for twenty years. A basket maker finds her in a bamboo grove and takes her home. He and his wife raise her, and she grows into a woman of unparalleled beauty. Eventually, after refusing several suitors (including the emperor), she returns to the moon. This netsuke shows the tiny princess wearing the robes of a noblewoman and sitting in a bamboo joint. The bamboo, carved to appear broken and damaged by insects, contrasts nicely with her finely finished features. On the underside, a budding branch and leaves form a natural *himotoshi*. Sōsui was the last artist of the Sō school, which began in the late 19th century with Miyazaki Josō (see cat. no. 206). Like other Sō carvers, he worked in both wood and ivory and found inspiration in the natural world. Here, he also used the *ukibori* technique for the raised patterns on the bamboo.

262

Dutchman, 20th century
Stag antler with mother-of-pearl,
glass, and gold inlays; 8.5 cm
Signed: *MHB* (Michael Birch, English, born 1926)

For this netsuke, the English artist Michael Birch relied on traditional Japanese depictions of Dutch traders with their exotic clothing, physiognomies, and hairstyles (see cat. nos. 33, 67, 68, 116, and 117). This Dutchman, carved to resemble Birch himself, wears a ruffed collar, knickers, and wooden shoes. The artist cleverly used the flaring shape and bumpy texture of the stag antler to render the man's short, woolly cape. He also capitalized on small imperfections in the material to suggest facial stubble and the stockings' texture. As is typical of his style, Birch embellished the work with discreet, yet well-integrated inlays of mother-of-pearl, glass, and gold.

263

Man lighting his pipe, 20th century
Wood with gold, horn, lacquer, and coral inlays; 4.3 cm
Signed: *Seihō* (Asuma Katsuo, born 1936)

Seihō began his career as an ivory carver, but made the majority of his works in wood. Although he usually depicts human figures, he also fashions *shishi* and a few other animals and birds. Here, he not only demonstrated his sophisticated carving skills but his ability to achieve subtle surface effects. He accented the wood with gold and black embellishments, including the man's *mon*, or family crest, on his kimono and lantern. The pipe also has gold fittings and red lacquer to suggest its glowing tobacco. The figure, dressed in traditional Japanese attire, wears a tobacco case with a coral *ojime* and a gourd netsuke.

264

Abalone diver and fish, mid-20th century
Wood, marine ivory, amber, and pearl; 6.8 cm
Signed: *Sōsui* (Ōuchi Jirō, 1911–72, Sō school, Tokyo)

In Japan, female divers (*ama*) have harvested abalone for centuries. The women, who wore only red skirts while diving, became frequent subjects for 19th-century woodblock and netsuke artists. Often, netsuke makers showed the divers in erotic embraces with various sea creatures, especially octopuses (see cat. no. 215). Sōsui created a number of carvings of female divers lying forlornly on dead fish. Here, the fish has been severed in two. Although his intention is not known, Sōsui might have viewed the diver herself as an amphibious creature, as powerless as the rest of the fisherman's catch.

265

Woman at rest, 20th century
Painted ivory; 5.5 cm
Signed: *Ryūshi* (Komada Isamu, born 1934)

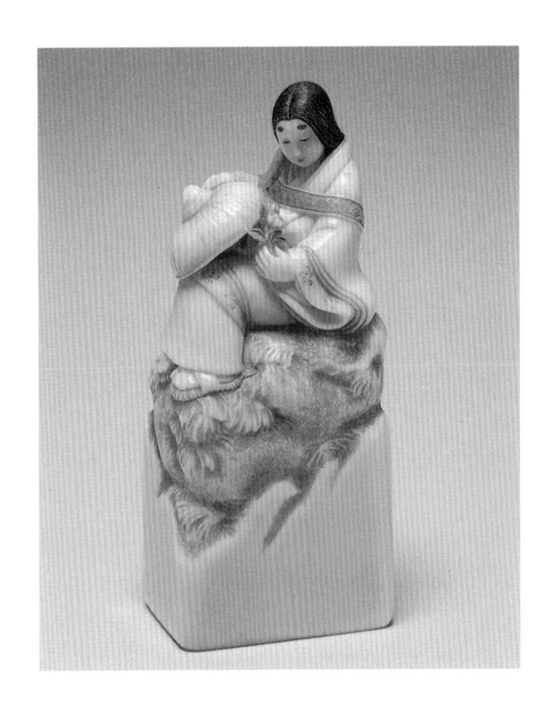

Ryūshi is famous for his historically accurate depictions of Japanese women from various periods. In this work, a maiden, holding a woven sun hat, wistfully admires a flower while sitting on a grassy knoll. Although the piece has not been inscribed, it can also function as a seal because of its rectangular base. Ryūshi's ancestors, like Shungetsu, started carving netsuke in the mid-19th century. Ryūshi first began his studies with his father, Komada Fukuichiro, who was a finish carver of decorative sculpture (*okimono*). While making *okimono*, Ryūshi taught himself netsuke production as well.

266

Butterfly Dancer/Madame Butterfly, 20th century
Painted wood; 9 cm
Signed: *DC* (David Carlin, American, born 1944)

David Carlin drew inspiration for this netsuke from two sources: the Japanese butterfly dance performed by children wearing colorful wings and Puccini's famous opera about a young Japanese woman, named Butterfly, who was seduced by an American naval officer. Carlin showed this Butterfly at the moment of her suicide—with the hilt of a long knife visible beneath her fan. Just as Butterfly set herself free from the sadness and disgrace of her abandonment, so, too, the butterflies here, which pattern her sash, magically come to life and fly away. Carlin graduated from the Society of Arts and Crafts in Detroit before moving to San Francisco, where he saw the Brundage netsuke collection at the Asian Art Museum. Since 1977, he has worked full-time as a netsuke carver.

267

Boy on a toy dog, 20th century
Painted ivory; 4.4 cm
Signed: *Ryūshi* (Komada Isamu, born 1934)

Although best known for his depictions of beautiful women (see cat. no. 265), Ryūshi has another favorite subject—children at play. This netsuke of a happy boy pretending to ride an *inubariko* probably commemorated the year of the dog. The Japanese make *inubariko* , brightly painted papier-mâché dogs, both as toys and protective talismans for children. Commonly purchased at Shinto shrines, *inubariko* supposedly trap evil and sickness in their hollow interiors. To make the vivid colors seen on this work, Ryūshi mixed natural pigments with a modern chemical adhesive, which produced a durable surface with a pleasing matte finish.

268

***Sanbasō* dancer**, early 20th century
Wood and ivory; 6.8 cm
Signed: *Kagetoshi* (school unknown)

A ritualistic dance sometimes performed at Nō plays, *Okina* (literally, "old man") involves three masked actors representing benevolent gods in the form of smiling old men. The final dance, known as *sanbasō,* features a comic Kyōgen actor who wears a black mask and holds a cluster of bells. The mask's dark color symbolizes earth and night, and the dance itself signifies prayers for an abundant harvest. In this netsuke, the artist used ebony for the dancer's black mask and persimmon wood for his tall lacquered hat. He included symbols for longevity (cranes, tortoises, and pines) on the figure's costume and minutely carved ivory for the mask's bushy eyebrows and beard. Ivory also represents the cords securing the mask's hinged jaw. The theme was carved as early as the mid-19th century by such Tokyo artists as Hōjitsu and Miyazaki Josō. This 20th-century example bears the art name Kagetoshi, a later artist who was undoubtedly inspired by those earlier renditions.

269

Skull, 20th century
Lacquered ivory; 4.3 cm
Signed with pictograph for "horse" (Okuda Kōdō, born 1940)

During the 15th century, the eccentric Zen priest Ikkyū paraded a human skull through the streets on New Year's Day to remind onlookers of their own inevitable demise. During the Edo period, Zen artists also used skulls symbolically to encourage people to attend to their own spiritual salvation. This contemporary rendition of a human skull follows that tradition and is all the more startling because of its astounding realism. Trained as a painter, Kōdō studied ivory carving with his father and lacquer production with Kuroda Tatsuaki. Here, he used *kanshitsu,* a specialized technique that produces soft, matte colors instead of the deep hues and shiny surfaces usually associated with lacquerwork.

270

Coiled dragon, 20th century

Ivory; 6 cm

Signed: *Ōsai* (Motomura Ōsai, 1908–85)

Self-taught, Ōsai produced netsuke, *okimono, obidome*, pins, and other carved adornments. Supposedly, he led a modest existence in the Kansai area and was so artistically isolated that he did not realize there were other carvers in Japan making netsuke until the early 1970s. This ivory dragon has the bulging eyes, horns, and streaming whiskers typically seen on such animals, particularly those embellishing the rafters and transoms of Buddhist temples. Ōsai, however, added a unique element by whimsically curling the beast's tail into a tight spiral. He also accentuated its complicated twisting by applying ink to the ridge of its back.

271

Metamorphosis, 20th century

Inrō: olive wood with gold leaf and inlay; 8 cm

Netsuke: mule deer antler with red and brown coral; 6.5 cm

Ojime: oosick and ox horn; 2.5 cm

Signed: *NL* (Nick Lamb, English, born 1948)

According to the artist, this ensemble illustrates the legend of the carp that was turned into a dragon to reward its persistence in climbing a waterfall. In both China and Japan, the carp symbolizes masculine determination and focused endeavor. During the Edo period, people with male children began flying carp-shaped banners (*koi-nobori*) from long bamboo poles on the fifth day of the fifth month. They associated that date with the presence of evil spirits, bad luck, and poisonous insects. To avert those calamities, parents encouraged their sons to engage in mock battles with wooden swords. Here, a variety of materials has been used to render the carp's mythical metamorphosis. The wooden inrō features the carp in relief, and the material's natural growth rings suggest rippling water. The small *ojime* also shows the animal still as a fish, whereas the netsuke pictures it in mid-transformation as the carp turns into a dragon.

272

***Kappa* in a leaf boat**, 20th century

Lacquered ivory, 6.2 cm

Signed with pictograph for "horse" (Okuda Kōdō, born 1940)

Kappa, or water sprites, are one of Kōdō's favorite subjects. In this netsuke, he stressed the creature's bucolic existence. Carved entirely from ivory, the tiny *kappa* here rides in a boat it has made from a bamboo leaf. Using a gourd as a sake decanter, it drinks a cup of the strong rice wine, adding to the pleasure of its idyllic cruise. Each of Kōdō's compositions is unique. Here, he used a specialized lacquer technique to give the object its soft, matte colors. Kōdō often signed his works *Bafunzan* (literally, "mountain of dung"), thus likening his prodigious output to horse droppings. For this netsuke, however, as well as catalogue number 269, he simply used the pictograph for horse.

273

***Kappa* in cucumber patch**, 20th century

Wood and ivory; 5.4 cm

Signed: *Ikku* (Isamu Kasuya, born 1949)

The top of this netsuke shows the bumpy leaves of a cucumber plant in astonishing detail, including insect damage. The underside, however, reveals a tiny *kappa*, which has gorged itself on cucumbers and fallen asleep. Imaginary water sprites, *kappa* have the bodies of turtles, the limbs of frogs, and the heads of monkeys. The depression on the top of their heads holds a small amount of life-giving water, allowing them to briefly leave the streams and rivers where they live to cause mischief and raid cucumber patches. The *kappa* here sleeps on its side, revealing its round, full stomach, while the cucumbers surrounding it have ragged bite marks. Ikku lives in Iruma City, near Tokyo. After first receiving a degree in design, he studied carving under Saitō Yasuo (Yasufusa), a cousin of Saitō Bishū. This work reveals Ikku's lively imagination and technical skill. The *ukibori* pimpling on the cucumber leaves has been especially well executed.

274

Nue, 20th century

Rhinoceros horn; 5 cm

Signed: *Masatoshi* (Nakamura Tokisada, born 1915)

According to Japanese mythology, *nue* have the heads of monkeys, the bodies of badgers, the tails of snakes, the claws of tigers, and the voices of birds. This unusual *nue* has a lion head with an ox body and hooves. It also has a goat head sprouting from its back that seems to converse with the lion head and the snake tail, which makes this creature more comical than frightening. Its maker, Masatoshi, learned netsuke carving from his father, Kuya, a sculptor of Buddhist imagery who began to craft netsuke in mid-career. Initially, Masatoshi produced detailed figure studies in ivory, but later on added animal subjects and, at the urging of his American patron Raymond Bushell, began to experiment with a variety of unusual materials. Here, he used rhinoceros horn, which is compressed and hardened hair.

275

Young *tengu* with *tengu* mask, 20th century

Ivory with inlay; 4 cm

Signed: *Masatoshi* (Nakamura Tokisada, born 1915)

Magical mountain goblins, *tengu* have the bodies of men and the heads and wings of birds. The oldest and most powerful *tengu* was Sōjōbō, who is usually depicted with an enormous nose instead of a beak. In this amusing example, a young *tengu* holds a mask of Sōjōbō and touches its nose in awe. Masatoshi, one of the "grand old men" of netsuke carving, has produced thousands of unique designs during his long career. The warm coloration of this ivory probably resulted from exposing it to incense smoke, a technique Masatoshi frequently uses.

276

Tiger, 20th century

Boxwood; 5 cm

Signed: *Bishū* (Saitō Bishū, born 1943)

The son of a commercial ivory carver, Bishū practiced that trade until the early 1970s, when he began to devote himself to more artistic renderings. To commemorate that decision, he adopted his art name Bishū, which means "beautiful country." While his choice of subject matter tends to be conventional, usually birds and animals, he does not replicate earlier designs. Instead, he makes his images distinctively contemporary (Kinsey, *Living Masters of Netsuke*, pp. 31–38). Here, he carved a tiger, skillfully capturing the sinuous grace of the rollicking beast with its head back, spine arched, and hindquarters in midair.

277

Paw prints in snow, 20th century

Ivory; 4.2 cm

Signed: *Risshisai Kangyoku* (Tachihara Noriyoshi, born 1944)

This unusual miniature has been carved to resemble the body of a dead rabbit blanketed with snow. The wolf prints on it ominously reveal how the rabbit met its fate. Reddish patches of fur on the netsuke's underside also suggest a bloody struggle. At the age of fifteen, Kangyoku began to learn carving from his father, Tachihara Fusakichi, a noted maker of ornamental ivory sculpture (*okimono*), who died when Kangyoku was only eighteen. Since finishing college, Kangyoku has operated a small netsuke studio in Urawa City, near Tokyo. While his works are always functional as netsuke, their subjects and designs are often highly innovative and, like this example, tend toward the abstract (Kinsey, *Living Masters of Netsuke*, pp. 17–30).

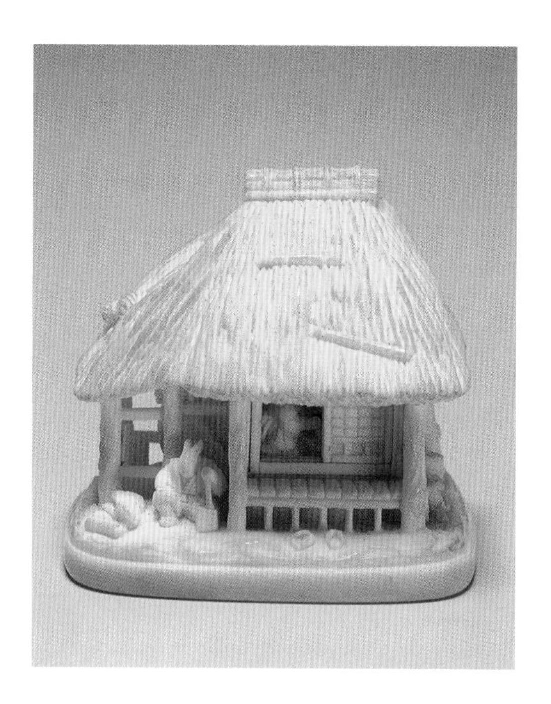

278

Cottage with monkey and rabbit, early 20th century
Ivory; 3.7 cm
Signed: *Kuya* (1881–1961)

Japanese artists have long delighted in rendering animals aping humans. In this netsuke, a hare and a monkey have set up house in a humble, thatched hut. The rabbit rests outside, ax in hand, while the monkey sits inside before a table laid out with cooking utensils. Kuya was trained to carve *okimono* (decorative sculpture), but began producing netsuke when he was forty. His works tend to be remarkable displays of minute and precise carving. In this case, the tiny cottage has doors that actually slide open and close. Kuya's son, Masatoshi (cat. nos. 274, 275, and 282), is also a highly respected netsuke maker.

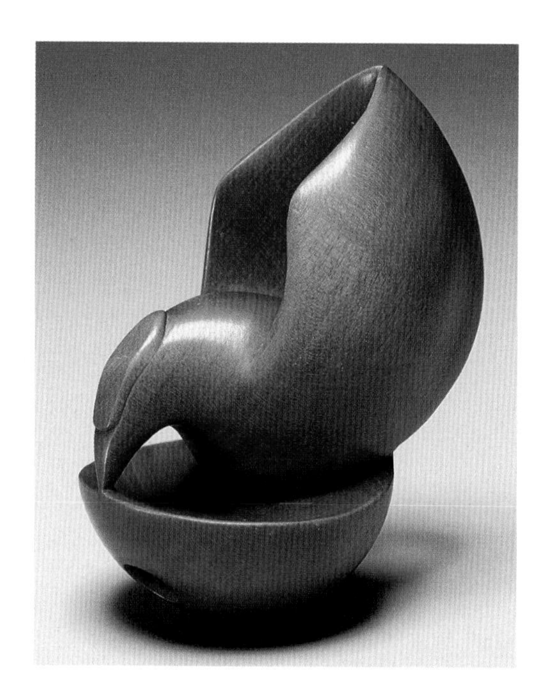

279

Bird, 20th century
Boxwood; 6 cm
Signed: *Bishū* (Saitō Bishū, born 1943)

Although trained as a commercial ivory carver, Bishū now makes netsuke in both ivory and wood as well as in more exotic materials. Throughout his career, he has striven to develop new and atypical poses for his animals and birds. The clean lines and abstract geometry of this work typify his designs and reflect both his study of historic netsuke and his awareness of such modern sculptors as Constantin Brancusi.

280

Crow, mid-20th century
Ebony and mother-of-pearl; 6.8 cm
Signed: *Sōsui* (Ōuchi Jirō, 1911–72, Sō school, Tokyo)

Sōsui appropriately chose ebony to render this stylized crow. He also hollowed the netsuke's interior and shaped the tail so it can be blown like a whistle. Sōsui was the son of Gyokusō, who was the pupil of Miyazaki Josō (see cat. 206), the founder of the Sō school of netsuke carvers in Tokyo. Gyokusō sent Sōsui as a young boy to study with fellow Sō artist Morita Sōko (see cat. no. 301). Like others of the Sō school, Sōsui preferred working in wood, but also carved ivory. He was best known for his complicated figural groups, especially of blind men in boats. This netsuke is unusual for him because of its simplified, contemporary style.

281

Heron in reeds, 20th century
Ivory with horn inlay; 6 cm
Signed: *Ikku* (Isamu Kasuya, born 1949)

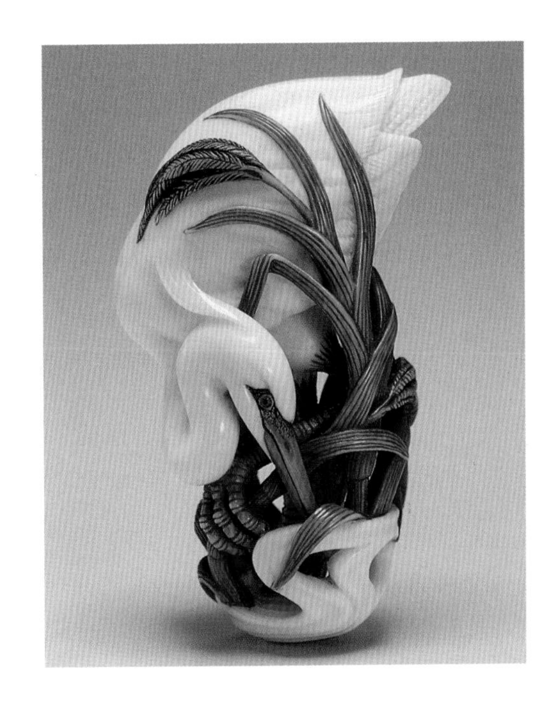

Ikku specializes in nature and animal subjects, which he finishes to a high degree. He uses a variety of materials, including boxwood, ebony, ivory, and stag antler, and often embellishes his carvings with inlays and lacquer. For this one, he created a dramatic impact by carefully staining the ivory to accent the heron's bill and legs and the surrounding reeds. His originality and technical finesse have made his netsuke extremely popular with collectors, even though he produces relatively few pieces.

282

Etopirika, 20th century

Hornbill beak with inlay; 6.8 cm

Signed: *Masatoshi ka* (Nakamura Tokisada, born 1915)

The highly versatile contemporary artist Masatoshi experiments with a wide variety of styles, techniques, and materials. His subjects range from finely detailed genre scenes to highly imaginative abstract forms. This netsuke portrays a kind of Japanese plover, which nests in cliffs along the seashore. The *etopirika*'s feathers are black, but its head turns white in summer with a slash of yellow over its eyes. Masatoshi ingeniously used part of a hornbill beak to portray the bird's dramatic coloration.

283

Two frogs in a rotting bucket, 20th century

Wood and ivory; 4.7 cm

Signed: *Kosei Hideyuki* (Sakurai Hideo, born 1941)

Hideyuki learned to carve from his father and then to sculpt at art school. Because his family once were ivory merchants, he initially worked in ivory. Later, however, he began to use wood and studied the techniques and netsuke of such Sō school artists as Sōko, Sōsui, and Shoko (Kinsey, *Living Masters of Netsuke*, pp. 39–46). Here, he displays his skill by finely rendering the grain of the wooden pail and by carefully reticulating the rope that drapes around its sides. As a whimsical addition, he placed two ivory frogs inside the bucket, seemingly locked in a romantic embrace.

284

Tree frog and spring apple, 20th century
Boxwood with inlay; 4.3 cm
Signed: *JJ* (Janel Jacobson, American, born 1950)

After attending Luther College in Iowa and studying with California potter Marguerite Wildenhain, Janel Jacobsen began her career as a potter in the 1970s. Her early production consisted of porcelain pots, plates, boxes, and tiles with carved designs and translucent celadon glazes. As she became more intrigued with sculptural forms, she also started to make porcelain netsuke. This finely detailed tree frog represents her first attempt at carving wood, which she undertook in 1995 with a piece of boxwood sent to her by artist Jim Kelso (see cat. no. 294). Her netsuke reflect her interest in the natural world, including frogs, insects, and various plant forms. She currently lives in rural Sunrise, Minnesota, working in a studio she shares with her potter husband, Will Swanson.

285

Tadpoles, 20th century
Wood with inlay; 4.8 cm
Signed: *SW* (Susan Wraight, Australian, born 1955)

Australian Susan Wraight first became aware of netsuke in 1978 while attending London's Royal College of Art, where she studied jewelry making. Inspired by the netsuke she saw at the Victoria and Albert Museum, she began fashioning her own. She draws inspiration from the natural world and favors animals and aquatic creatures as her subjects. Lately, she has also created works based on Western myths and legends, like Aesop's *Fables*. Her initial theme for this netsuke was water, but she found it impossible to capture its liquid qualities in wood. She cleverly solved the problem by depicting tadpoles instead, whose long, sweeping tails aptly convey the water's swirling presence.

286

Snail on driftwood, 20th century
Ivory, wood, and lacquer; 11 cm
Signed with pictograph for "horse" (Okuda Kōdō, born 1940)

Kōdō lives in the countryside, away from the urban sprawl of nearby Tokyo. His garden has a small stream that often provides inspiration for his designs. Before beginning a new project, he spends considerable time studying his subject. Here, he portrayed a snail on a piece of driftwood. He carved the creature from a single piece of ivory, then skillfully colored its spiraling shell and antenna. He accentuated the ivory's creamy color by placing it against the rich stain of the wood.

287

Turtle and seaweed, 20th century
Fossilized walrus ivory with inlay; 6 cm
Signed: *GS* (Gregg Stradiotto, American, born 1949)

A lifelong carver, Gregg Stradiotto first began crafting netsuke after seeing the Brundage collection in San Francisco at the Asian Art Museum. While always making compact netsuke designs, Stradiotto often renders images that are non-Japanese in theme, frequently incorporating his knowledge of Western sculpture and North American wildlife into his works. He also freely experiments with different materials. For this netsuke, he used his favorite medium—fossilized walrus ivory, showing its subtle color variations and glassy translucency to great advantage.

288

Lobster, 20th century
Wood with coral inlay; 5 cm
Signed: *MW* (Michael Webb, English, born 1934)

Michael Webb first became interested in netsuke in 1967, when he was working as an auctioneer in London at Sotheby's and the Hindson netsuke collection was sold there. Since that time, he has made a career as a carver, working almost exclusively in wood. Most of his designs feature animals or insects, and he may very well be the first non-Japanese artist to master the specialized technique of *ukibori*. Here, he used the method to suggest the rough texture of a lobster's exoskeleton.

289

Inrō, netsuke, and *ojime* with shrimp motif, 20th century
Inrō: glazed ceramic; 6 cm
Netsuke: glazed ceramic; 5.1 cm
Ojime: glazed ceramic; 3.5 cm
Obidome: glazed ceramic; 8.25 cm
Signed with ideograph for "water"
(Armin Müller, American, born 1932)

Early in his career, potter Armin Müller made small porcelain storage jars for powdered tea (*chaire*). For the lids, he asked David Carlin (see cat. no. 266) to sculpt tiny decorative knobs out of clay. With Carlin's encouragement, Müller eventually began to make the knobs himself. In the late 1980s, he also started crafting netsuke after seeing them on display at San Francisco's Asian Art Museum. He investigated the Edo period's production of ceramic netsuke, *ojime*, and inrō and continues to expand on those traditions. Here, he created a man's *sagemono* ensemble with a matching *obidome*, a clasp worn by women in the center of their wide sashes. To provide a dramatic background for his brightly colored shrimp, he glazed the porcelain black. He also pitted the surface to resemble the rough texture of stone (*ishime*). He further enlivened the composition by picturing the shrimps' curving feelers and giving the crustaceans staring comical eyes.

290

Fish head, 20th century

Wood with horn inlay; 4 cm

Signed: *Rei* (Geijo Reigen, born 1935)

Reigen was trained as a decorative transom carver, but subsequently became a Tokyo businessman. He began to carve netsuke as a hobby in 1974, working almost exclusively in wood. His reclusive personality has prevented him from becoming better known. He does not participate in netsuke exhibitions and is not a member of any Japanese carving society. He draws his subjects from nature and is particularly fond of portraying fish. For this work, he captured the grotesque appearance of a grouper, contrasting its pitted, bumpy skin against its smooth, cartilaginous mouth.

291

Carp and coin, 20th century

Stag antler with inlay; 4.5 cm

Signed: *GS* (Guy Shaw, English, born 1951)

Guy Shaw initially trained as a painter and lithographer before turning to sculpture. He first became interested in netsuke during the early 1980s and began carving them with the help and encouragement of his friend Michael Birch, who is also a netsuke artist (see cat. nos. 258 and 262). Shaw frequently uses novel materials for his works, often creating images with metaphorical content. He has said that the carp here represents humanity's spirit imprisoned by greed, symbolized by the coin.

292

Seaweed seahorse, 20th century
Mammoth ivory with coral inlay; 6 cm
Signed: *GS* (Guy Shaw, English, born 1951)

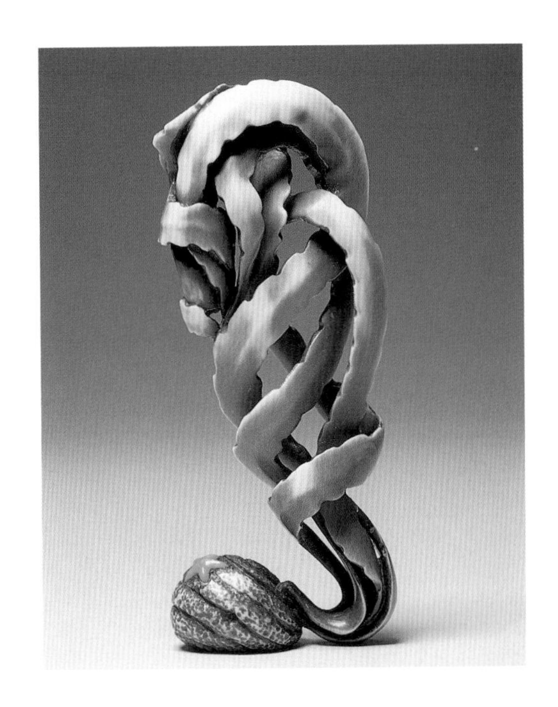

Since the 1989 international ban on the sale and transport of elephant ivory, artists have used mammoth ivory instead, which comes from fossil beds. For this elegant work, Guy Shaw carved the material to resemble a weightless tangle of kelp. Shaped like a seahorse, it seems to be emerging from a seashell. Shaw tinted the ivory blue to suggest the ocean's great depth.

293

Two cicadas, 20th century
Ivory; 4.5 cm
Signed: *Senpo* (Iriyama Senkichi, 1919–94)

Senpo learned to carve from his father, Buichiro, a professional ivory *arabori-shi* (rough-cut craftsman), who turned his works over to other artists for finishing. Although Senpo became aware of various netsuke techniques from his contemporaries, he remained largely self-taught. As a boy, he had lost his hearing and later in life suffered from a degenerative nerve disorder that left one side of his face paralyzed. Despite those challenges, he became a superb carver, specializing in closely observed portrayals of animals and insects (Comee, "The Genius of Senpo," pp. 10–23).

294

***Kagamibuta* netsuke with spider**, 20th century
Stag antler, horn, silver, copper, and gold; 4.8 cm
Signed: *JK* (Jim Kelso, American, born 1950)

Originally, American Jim Kelso trained to build boats and to construct musical instruments. Later, he turned his expertise in metalworking to forging decorative hilts, handles, and scabbards for Japanese-style swords. After receiving a fellowship to study in Japan in 1987, he increasingly made netsuke and *ojime*. For this *kagamibuta* netsuke, he combined an old stag-antler bowl with a metal disk he fabricated, which depicts a spider crawling across pine bark. To display his knowledge of metal alloys, he also used *shibuichi* (an amalgam of silver and copper) for the bark, patinated silver for the pine needles, copper for the branch, and gold for the spider and tree lichen.

295

Bamboo shoot, mid-20th century
Wood; 5.8 cm
Signed: *Sōsui* (Ōuchi Jirō, 1911–72, Sō school, Tokyo)

Sō school artists specialized in painstakingly rendered images of natural subjects. In this netsuke, Sōsui reproduced a bamboo shoot with great botanical accuracy, showing the root nodes at its base and how the sheaths overlap and curl at the edges. He used a natural opening in the husk for the *himotoshi*. The Japanese consider bamboo shoots, which appear in spring, to be culinary delicacies.

296

Morning glories, 20th century
Wood, horn, coral, and mother-of-pearl; 5 cm
Signed: *Shūbi* (born 1916)

The Japanese associate certain plants with specific months and seasons. Although morning glories bloom all summer long, they are usually linked with the heat of August. This netsuke of a bucket overgrown with flower vines was inspired by a famous haiku by the female poet Fukuda Chiyo'ni (1701–75), which reads:

> A morning glory,
> Having taken my well bucket,
> I begged for water.

The artist Shūbi is best known for his finely carved boxwood netsuke, which he finishes with a light orange stain. For this example, he accented the composition with small bits of inlay.

297

Three Friends of Winter (*Shochikubai*), 20th century
Ivory, gold, semiprecious stones, and tortoiseshell; 11 cm
Signed: *Hideyuki* (Sakurai Hideo, born 1941)

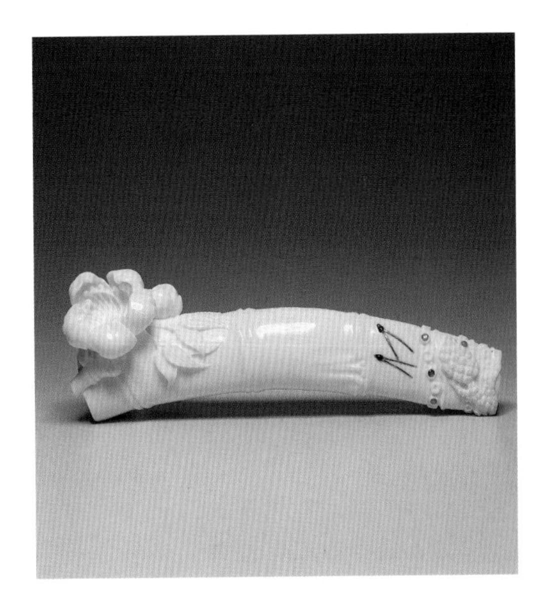

In both China and Japan, the blossoming plum, bamboo, and pine, known as the "three friends of winter," symbolize resiliency in the face of hardship. The plum tree is the first to blossom in the spring, sometimes while snow still covers its branches. The bamboo bends in the fierce winter winds, but does not break. And the pine, an evergreen, can live for centuries. For this *sashi* netsuke, Hideyuki fashioned a length of bamboo with a spray of plum blossoms at one end and pine cones at the other. For additional embellishment and opulence, he used gold wire for the pine needles, inlaying them and the bamboo nodes with a variety of small, semiprecious stones.

298

Lacquered box with two inrō, 20th century

Wood, lacquer, mother-of-pearl, gold stone, and ivory; 4.5 cm

Signed: *Shūbi* (born 1916)

Netsuke artists usually portray humans or animals. But here, Shūbi made a miniaturized set of netsuke and inrō in a tiny storage box. He carved the netsuke and inrō ensembles from ivory and then painted them with red and black lacquer. He crafted the box, with its grapevine motif and sprinkled gold background, from lacquer. The three additional "button" shapes in the box represent spare netsuke. This work signals a departure for Shūbi, who is best known for his floral studies carved from boxwood (see cat. no. 296).

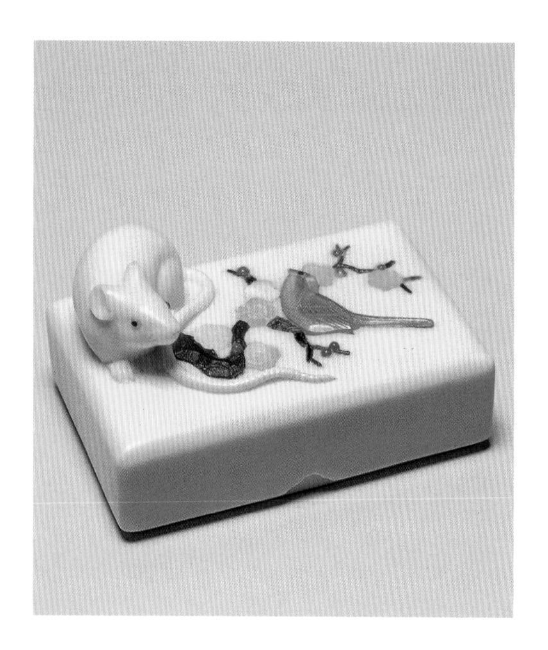

299

Precious Things (*Kichō*), 20th century

Ivory with mother-of-pearl, tortoiseshell, coral, jadeite, and horn inlays; 4.5 cm

Signed: *Yasufusa* (Saitō Yasuo, born 1931)

This netsuke represents a *suzuribako,* a writing box designed to hold a brush, ink stone, and ink stick. The blossoming plum symbolizes spring and is used on New Year's decorations to signify renewal. The rat's inclusion on the box might indicate the year the netsuke was made.

300

***Go* board**, 20th century

Lacquer and wood; 4.3 cm

Signed: *Tomizō* (Saratani Tomizō, born 1949)

The Japanese aristocracy began playing *go* in the 8th century. During the Edo period, however, all classes of Japanese society enjoyed the Chinese game. To compete, players used a checkered board and small white and black stones. The *go* board, a thick block of wood on small legs, was often elaborately ornamented. This netsuke portrays a lacquered *go* board. Its sides have been decorated with blossoming plants, which represent the four seasons. Saratani Tomizō, who currently resides in Hokkaidō, was trained as a lacquer artist and has worked as a professional lacquer conservator. He has also lived in London, Vienna, New York, and Chicago, experiences that encouraged him to experiment artistically. His netsuke, inrō, and *ojime* designs often serve as outlets for his creativity.

301

Tangerine box, early 20th century

Boxwood and ivory; 4.5 cm

Signed: *Sōko* (Morita Sōko, 1879–1942)

A pupil of the founder of the Sō school (see cat. no. 206), Sōko was an important teacher in his own right, having trained Shoko and Sōsui (cat. nos. 261, 264, 280, and 295). Like other Sō artists, Sōko carved both wood and ivory and used nature as the starting point for his compositions. In particular, he gained admiration for his fantastically detailed flower studies. This netsuke shows his ability to transform even the most mundane subject into a compelling design. Here, he sculpted a wooden crate held together with heavy rope. He carefully rendered the crate's rough planks and the rope's hemp fibers. As a foil to the box's rigid regularity, he masterfully revealed the soft, round tangerines it contains.

INDEX

All numbers refer to catalogue numbers.

Artists

Schools

Specialized Forms and Unusual Materials

Subjects

Addiss, Stephen. *The Art of Zen.* New York: Harry N. Abrams, 1989.

———, ed. *Japanese Ghosts and Demons, Art of the Supernatural.* New York: George Braziller, 1985.

Arakawa, Hirokazu. *Gō Collection of Netsuke.* Tokyo: Kodansha International, 1983.

Barker, Richard, and Lawrence Smith. *Netsuke: The Miniature Sculpture of Japan.* rev. ed. Barron's Educational Series. London: British Museum, 1979.

Bellah, Robert N. *Tokugawa Religion.* Boston: Beacon Press, 1957.

British Museum and the Los Angeles County Museum of Art. *Treasured Miniatures: Contemporary Netsuke.* Tokyo: Ribun, 1994.

Brockhaus, Albert. *Netsuke: Versuch einer Geschichte der Japanischen Schnitzkunst.* Leipzig: Albert Brockhaus, 1905. Reprint, 1909 and 1924.

———. *Netsukes.* Translated by M. F. Watty and edited by E. G. Stillman. Based on the 1924 German edition. New York: Hacker Art Books, 1969.

Brown, Kendall. "Why Art Historians Don't Study Netsuke, and Why They Should." *International Netsuke Society Journal* 17, no. 1 (spring 1997): 8–24.

Bushell, Raymond. *The Netsuke Handbook of Ueda Reikichi.* Adopted from *Netsuke no kenkyū* by Ueda Reikichi. Tokyo and Rutland, Vt.: Charles E. Tuttle Co., 1961.

———. *Netsuke Familiar and Unfamiliar: New Principles for Collecting.* New York and Tokyo: John Weatherhill, 1975.

———. *Collectors' Netsuke.* New York and Tokyo: John Weatherhill, 1977.

———. *The Inro Handbook: Studies of Netsuke, Inro, and Lacquer.* New York and Tokyo: John Weatherhill, 1979.

Clark, Timothy. *Ukiyo-e Paintings in the British Museum.* Washington, D.C.: Smithsonian Institution Press, 1992.

Cohen, George. *In Search of Netsuke and Inro.* Birmingham, England: Jacey Group of Companies, 1974.

Comee, Stephen. "The Genius of Senpo: A Love Song to Nature." *Netsuke Kenkyukai Study Journal* 14, no. 3 (fall 1994): 10–23.

Coullery, Marie-Thérèse, and Martin S. Newstead. *The Baur Collection: Netsuke.* Geneva: Collections Baur-Genève, 1977.

Davey, Neil K. *Netsuke: A Comprehensive Study Based on the M. T. Hindson Collection.* rev. ed. New York: Sotheby Publications, 1982.

Davey, Neil K., and Susan G. Tripp. *The Garrett Collection, Japanese Art: Lacquer, Inro, Netsuke.* London: Dauphin Publishing, 1993.

De Visser, M. N. "The Snake in Japanese Superstition." *Ostasiatische Studien* 14 (1911).

Ducros, Alain. *Netsuke et Sagemono.* Lyons, France: Alain Ducros, 1987.

———. "Sokei." *Netsuke Kenkyukai Study Journal* 12, no. 3 (fall 1992): 21–25.

Edmunds, Will H. *Pointers and Clues to the Subjects of Chinese and Japanese Art.* London: Sampson, Low, Marston and Co., 1934. Reprint, Geneva: Minkoff, 1974.

French, Calvin. *Through Closed Doors: Western Influences in Japanese Art, 1639–1853.* Rochester, Mich.: Meadowbrook Art Gallery, 1977.

Hall, John Whitney, ed. *Early Modern Japan.* vol. 4 of *The Cambridge History of Japan.* Cambridge: Cambridge University Press, 1991.

Hopkins, Jay E. "Early Elephant Ivory Netsuke." *Netsuke Kenkyukai Study Journal* 2, no. 2 (1982): 7–18.

Hurtig, Bernard. *Masterpieces of Netsuke Art.* New York and Tokyo: John Weatherhill, 1973.

Hutt, Julia. *Japanese Inrō.* London: Victoria and Albert Museum, 1997.

Ihara, Saikaku. *Koshoku ichidai otoko.* Annotated by Fuji Akio and Asō Isoji. vol. 1 of *Ketteisho taiyu Saikaku zenshu.* Tokyo: Seibunsha, 1992.

———. *Nanshoku okagami.* Annotated by Fuji Akio and Asō Isoji. vol. 6 of *Ketteisho taiyu Saikaku zenshu.* Tokyo: Seibunsha, 1992.

International Netsuke Society Journal 16–18 (1996–98).

Jahss, Melvin, and Betty Jahss. *Inro and Other Miniature Forms of Japanese Lacquer Art.* Tokyo and Rutland, Vt.: Charles E. Tuttle Co., 1971.

Jansen, Marius B., and Gilbert Rozman, eds. *Japan in Transition: From Tokugawa to Meiji.* Princeton, N.J.: Princeton University Press, 1986.

Joly, Henri L. *Legend in Japanese Art.* London: John Lane, 1908. Reprint, Tokyo and Rutland, Vt.: Charles E. Tuttle Co., 1967.

Jonas, F. M. *Netsuke.* London: Kegan Paul, Trench, Trubner and Co., 1928. Reprint, Tokyo and Rutland, Vt.: Charles E. Tuttle Co., 1960.

Journal of the International Netsuke Collectors Society 1–12 (1973–85).

Kamens, Edward. "Translations of Teika's Poems." In *Word in Flower*, edited by Carolyn Wheelwright. New Haven, Conn.: Yale University Art Gallery, 1989.

Kazaaru korekushon: Netsuke. vol. 11 in *Osaka shiritsu bijutsukan shohin zuroku.* Osaka: Osaka Shiritsu Bijutsukan, 1982.

Keyes, Roger. *The Art of Surimono: Privately Published Japanese Woodblock Prints and Books in the Chester Beatty Library, Dublin.* 2 vols. London: Sotheby, 1985.

Kinsey, Miriam. *Contemporary Netsuke.* Tokyo and Rutland, Vt.: Charles E. Tuttle Co., 1977.

———. *Living Masters of Netsuke.* Tokyo: Kodansha International, 1984.

Kinsey, Robert, and Miriam Kinsey. *Contemporary Netsuke: Miniature Sculpture from Japan and Beyond.* Santa Ana, Calif.: Bowers Museum of Cultural Art, 1997.

Klefisch, Trudel. *Netsuke, Inro und andere Sagemono.* Cologne: Museum für Ostasiatische Kunst, 1982.

Kodansha Encyclopedia of Japan. 9 vols. Tokyo: Kodansha International, 1983.

Kurstin, Joseph. "Seventeenth-Century Netsuke." *Netsuke Kenkyukai Study Journal* 15, no. 1 (spring 1995): 44–58.

Lazarnick, George. *Netsuke and Inro Artists, and How to Read Their Signatures.* 2 vols. Honolulu: Reed Publishers, 1982.

London Netsuke Committee. *Contrasting Styles, A Loan Exhibition of Netsuke and Kiseruzutsu from Private English Collections.* London: Robert G. Sawers Publishing, 1980.

Masatoshi. *The Art of Netsuke Carving.* As told to Raymond Bushell. Tokyo: Kodansha International, 1981.

Meinertzhagen, Frederick. *The Art of the Netsuke Carver.* London: Routledge and Kegan Paul, 1956.

———. *The Art of the Netsuke Carver.* Hollywood, Fla.: Kurstin-Schneider, 1975.

———. *MCI: The Meinertzhagen Card Index on Netsuke in the Archives of the British Museum.* Edited by George Lazarnick. New York: Alan R. Liss, 1986.

Mirviss, Joan, and John Carpenter. *The Frank Lloyd Wright Collection of Surimono.* New York: Weatherhill; Phoenix: Phoenix Art Museum, 1995.

Netsuke: Edo saimitsu kogei no hana. Kanagawa: Netsuke Kenkyukai, 1995.

Netsuke Kenkyukai Study Journal 1–15 (1981–95).

Nishiyama, Matsunosuke. *Edo Culture: Daily Life and Diversions in Urban Japan, 1600–1868.* Translated and edited by Gerald Groemer. Honolulu: University of Hawaii Press, 1997.

Okada, Barbra Teri. *Netsuke: Masterpieces from the Metropolitan Museum of Art.* New York: Metropolitan Museum of Art and Harry N. Abrams, 1982.

Okada, Barbra Teri, and Mary Gardner Neill. *Real and Imaginary Beings: The Netsuke Collection of Joseph and Edith Kurstin.* New Haven, Conn.: Yale University Art Gallery, 1980.

Okada, Yuzuru. *Netsuke—A Miniature Art of Japan.* vol. 14 of *Tourist Library.* Tokyo: Japan Travel Bureau, 1951. Reprint, 1953.

Ryerson, Egerton. *The Netsuke of Japan: Legends, History, Folklore and Customs.* London: Thomas Yoseloff; New York: A. S. Barnes and Co., 1958.

Sansom, George B. *A History of Japan: 1615–1867.* Stanford, Calif.: Stanford University Press, 1963.

———. *Japan: A Short Cultural History.* Tokyo and Rutland, Vt.: Charles E. Tuttle Co., 1985.

Shibusawa, Keizō, comp. and ed. *Japanese Life and Culture in the Meiji Era.* Translated by Charles S. Terry. Centenary Culture Council Series. Tokyo: Ōbunsha, 1958.

Tsuda, Sukesada. *Ichi-i ittobori.* Tokyo: Jitsubō, 1986.

Ueda, Reikichi. *Netsuke no kenkyū.* Kanao Bunbuchidō, 1943.

Volker, T. *The Animal in Far Eastern Art and Especially in the Art of the Japanese Netsuke.* rev. ed. Leiden, Netherlands: E. J. Brill, 1975.

Yanagida, Kunio, comp. and ed. *Japanese Manners and Customs in the Meiji Era.* Translated and adapted by Charles S. Terry. Centenary Culture Council Series. Tokyo: Ōbunsha, 1957.